Praise for *Why Not Be a Prodigal*

Finally, a book that Christian teens can easily relate too and pass along to their friends who may be struggling in the real world. Allen Webster takes young people "where they need to go" in a way they will appreciate and learn from. *Why Not Be a Prodigal* tackles tough topics in a fresh, straightforward, and biblical fashion. It covers the spectrum of real temptations facing young people today—delivering wisdom from both the Old and New Testament. I am already looking for space on my bookshelf, as this book will find a permanent place in our home for my own children. At a time when the church is begging for solid and sound teen material, *Why Not Be a Prodigal* answers the call. Having surveyed thousands of young Christian college students—many of whom are struggling with their faith and temptations—this book is a "must" for Bible classes all across our country.

—BRAD HARRUB
Editor, *Think* Magazine

Why Not Be A
Prodigal?

ALLEN WEBSTER

First Printing 2008

ISBN 978-1-60644-025-4

ATTENTION CHURCHES, UNIVERSITIES, COLLEGES, AND ORGANIZATIONS: Quantity discounts are available on bulk purchases of this book for educational and gift purposes, or as premiums for increasing magazine subscriptions or renewals. Special books or book excerpts can also be created to suit specific needs. For more information, please contact Heart to Heart Publishing Inc., PO Box 520, Jacksonville, AL 36265. Phone: 256–435–9356.

Web site: htpp://www.housetohouse.com/.

Dedicated to my children:
Rosa
Daniel
David
Lois

God's special treasures that live at our address,
whom we hope to send back to live with Him in a few years.

Table of Contents

Foreword:
A Parable Jesus Never Told

Once upon a time there was a church looking toward the future. Some members were concerned for the spiritual welfare of the youth growing up in an immoral, decadent age. They created a plan to encourage a thirst for righteousness among their young (Matthew 5:6) and to fortify their faith so they could withstand the devil's onslaught (Ephesians 6:13–18; 1 Peter 5:8).

First, the planners decided they needed a strong Bible teaching program. The Scriptures produce faith (Romans 10:17), cleanse a young man's way (Psalm 119:9, 11), defeat the devil's temptations (Matthew 4:1–11), and provide answers to life's big questions (2 Peter 1:3). The church would need knowledgeable, capable, caring teachers for youth classes (Romans 10:14; 2 Timothy 2:2). So they tried to recruit good teachers. They were surprised by the resistance they met.

One person said, "I don't want to leave the fellowship of my adult class to teach children."

But the drug pusher said, "Not even the threat of jail will keep me from working with your children" (cf. Romans 6:13).

Another responded, "I don't know enough to teach children about God."

But the evolutionists went to college to learn how to teach children that there is no God (Psalm 14:1).

Another replied, "Young people today are so different. I could never keep their attention."

But movie producers said, "We'll study, survey, and spend millions to produce whatever turns kids on" (cf. Psalm 101:3).

Second, the planners recognized that "teachers cannot educate if children vacate." So they talked with parents about making a commitment to have their children in every Bible class. Surely, this would be easier. After all, a parent's greatest responsibility is to a child's spiritual welfare (Ephesians 6:4; Deuteronomy 6:7; Proverbs 22:6; Genesis 18:19).

Some parents excused themselves saying, "We're out of town too often on weekends, and everybody's tired on Wednesdays."

But the porno book dealer said, "We'll stay open late every night and especially weekends to accommodate your children" (Matthew 5:28; cf. Philippians 4:8).

Another said, "Two classes a week is too big a commitment." (The same parent committed to have the same children in public school five days a week.)

But fashion designers and cosmetics companies committed millions to teach children to emphasize the outward man and dress in worldly fashions (cf. 1 Timothy 2:9–10).

Third, the planners decided that it would help to have devotionals, youth meetings, Bible bowls, retreats, and other outings for the youth. This would require adults to volunteer their homes, drive from place to place, fix snacks, and give of themselves. The planners thought, "It's for a good cause; young people are important."

Church leaders said, "It is expensive to pay for speakers, provide Bibles, literature, and food for so many. It costs too much."

But beer and cigarette companies said, "We'll advertise on every radio and TV station. We'll entice from billboards and magazines. It pays to advertise."

Some complained, "We're too busy to fool with youth activities. Let them find their own things to do. We don't want to be bothered."

But the school organized and promoted dances for the children (cf. Galatians 5:19–21).

Others said, "I don't want to chaperone teens to youth meetings. Gas is expensive, plus I have to consider the wear on my vehicle. Besides, I try to go to bed early."

But the casino operators promised to shuttle the youth from convenient locations all over the city so they can have the opportunity to gamble (1 Timothy 6:10; cf. Romans 12:17).

Another told them, "I couldn't host a devotional at my house. Those little monsters might break something. Plus, it would be a lot of trouble to clean up when it was over."

But the city let a popular rock band come to the civic center to entertain the youth and even provided city cleanup crews when it was over (cf. Proverbs 4:23, 26).

So the adults stayed in their adult classes, young people slept in, parents stayed busy until their children grew up, families went out of town on weekends, and the youth group was inactive. But the drug dealers, porn salesmen, movie producers, gamblers, schools, and tobacco and liquor manufacturers worked hard, spent money, and did what was necessary to win the impressionable minds of the kids. They all claimed great success.

The planners were reminded of Jesus' Parable of the Unjust Steward. In it He said, "The children of this world are in their generation wiser than the children of light" (Luke 16:8).

One Sunday came when the adults wondered why the youth classes were empty. Some complained, "This church sure is dead. Nothing but gray heads around here." Parents wondered why they could not get their children to go to worship. Others asked, "What has happened to this younger generation?"

"He that hath ears to hear, let him hear" (Matthew 11:15).

The Far Country Will Teach You More Than You Want to Know

Lesson text: Genesis 3; Luke 15:11-32

Memory verse: "Good understanding giveth favour: but the way of transgressors is hard" (Proverbs 13:15).

Many young people who grow up in Christian families believe the prodigal son had a good idea. When they hit the mid-to-late-teen years, they decide to take a vacation from God. Experience sin. Taste alcohol. Smoke a few cigarettes. Dance at the prom. Watch some dirty movies. Hit the college night spots. Maybe get high—once, just to know what it feels like. Get wild on Spring Break and graduation night. Experiment with parking, petting . . . get serious with a boyfriend or girlfriend and "go all the way." Sow some wild oats. Give the devil his due. After all, "You're only young once."

Then, the thinking goes, "I'll come back to God later. I'm not going to stay away from church. About the time I get married, or at least when I have a child, I'll come back home. Repent. Start over. No harm done. Heaven and all that."

In other words, "Sin now; repent later."

Is there anything wrong with this "best of both worlds" approach to life? Did God put Luke 15 in the Bible to encourage teens to follow the prodigal into the far country? No, this game plan never came from God; it is straight out of the devil's playbook.

What's Wrong with Experimenting with the Prodigal Lifestyle?

Signing up for the course

One of the devil's sales pitches is as old as Eden: "You mean you haven't tried it?" Friends may ask, "You've never tasted beer? You've never smoked a cigarette? You've never worn (or watched) a bikini on the beach? You've never gone to a wild party? You've never seen an R-rated movie? You've never shoplifted? You've never been high? You're the last virgin in our school?" Many young people, like Eve, stupidly fall for the serpent's line. Sure, you'll get an education—but you'll stay after school, put in long hours of homework, and work on weekends to get it. You'll wish you'd never signed up.

Ask Eve.

The first test

In a way, Eve was in her teen years. We are not sure how much time had passed since creation, but she was facing her first test with the devil—much like teens. The first sin in Eden, then, is typical of many first sins now, in the sense of deliberate disobedience of God's known will. Of course, we sinned through ignorance and weakness many times before "taking a prodigal trip," but presumptuous or deliberate sins are far worse. David asked to be kept back "from presumptuous sins; let them not have dominion over me" (Psalm 19:13).

The devil played on Eve's innocence. He made her feel that she was missing out because she had not experienced sin. He implied that she did not know enough. "For God doth know that in the day ye eat thereof, then your eyes shall be opened, and ye shall be as gods, knowing good and evil"

(Genesis 3:5). One of the things that made the tree "to be desired" was that it would "make one wise" (3:6)—that is, it would increase one's knowledge.

And as soon as Eve and Adam ate the fruit, their eyes "were opened, and they knew" (Genesis 3:7). They had expanded their education. They knew things they hadn't known before. What things? Not the things the devil said they would know. They were not more like God. (They had been made "in His image," 1:27; now, with sin-sullied souls, they were less like Him). They had already known that obeying God was good and disobeying God was evil.

What things, then, did they know post-sin that they did not know pre-sin? They knew shame (they realized they were naked, 3:7) and guilt (they hid from God, 3:8). For the first time, they knew separation from God (3:8), fear of God (3:9–10), and punishment from God (3:16–19). They didn't enjoy what they learned from sin.

The class party: Drinking will teach you more than you want to know

Today sin still teaches young people all about shame, guilt, and punishment. Consider the temptation to drink alcohol. Someone at the class party asks, "You mean you've never had a drink? You don't know what you're missing." True, but there are some things you don't want to know, as Adam and Eve discovered the hard way.

One thousand American teens started drinking today—365,000 will begin this year. If you are one of them, alcohol is sure to give you an education. You'll have Nausea 101 and Hangover 201. You may take a course in Wrecked Car and Bad Grades. You'll likely get a degree in Embarrassment and may take a minor in Fighting and Breakup. Many graduate to Binge, then attend Addiction U., and they usually take some graduate courses in Relapse. Some continue their education until they finish with a doctorate in Cirrhosis and Cemetery.

Won't ever happen to me, you say? So does every other teen who starts drinking. Look around at the next party and count nine others. Statistically, one of you will be an alcoholic, and three or four of you will be "problem drinkers." And guess how many will end up in heaven.

Stop and read some Scriptures on God's view of alcohol: Genesis 9:21–24; Proverbs 20:1; 23:29–35; Matthew 24:49; Galatians 5:21; Ephesians 5:18.

Private lessons: Sex will teach you more than you want to know

Sex will give you an education, too. The tests in this course can be really hard. They go in a similar pattern to Eve's: shame, guilt, separation from God (even if one continues to "go to church," singing "Nearer My God to Thee" lacks something), fear of getting caught, a bad reputation, loss of self-respect, worry over pregnancy, thoughts of suicide.

Of course, punishment from God ultimately follows if one doesn't repent and cease (Romans 2:9, 11; 2 Corinthians 5:10; Galatians 5:19, 21). In the meantime, there often come the difficult decisions of what to do with an unwanted child, a long hard life of trying to finish high school or college while caring for a child, changing dirty diapers, paying expenses such as food and medical bills, and missing many of the "fun" things other young people are doing.

Getting ready for marriage? Many teens have the mistaken idea that they will be a disappointment to their future spouses if they don't know anything about being a sexual partner on their wedding night. The opposite is true. Your partner wants to learn *with* you, not *from* you. If you know more than your mate, then he or she will wonder how you learned. Your mate will fight feelings of jealousy and insecurity.

A teacher had twelve students in his class. He brought into the room a box of thirteen roses. Taking one of them out of the box, he passed it around the class, asking each student to feel its texture and smell its fragrance. Afterwards, he placed it back into the box with the others. When the class period came to a close, he passed the box of roses around the room for each student to get one to keep. With twelve students and thirteen roses, naturally one would be left. Which do you suppose it was? It was the one everybody had touched—the one whose petals were falling off that did not look very fresh anymore.

In like manner, we urge all of our young people to avoid becoming used and soiled. Rather, we encourage them to preserve their chastity and purity at all costs, giving themselves to one man or one woman for life.

The stakes are high. In the United States, about 2,800 teen girls get pregnant each day—nearly one million young women under age twenty become pregnant each year. Every day, 1,106 make the wrong decision to kill the baby by abortion. Every day, 2,200 teens drop out of school, many of them because of pregnancy.

Even if you and your spouse are both experienced, it is a detriment to your sexual relationship rather than an asset to it. Do you want to marry someone with a sexually transmitted disease? If you are sexually active, you may be one of 4,219 American teens who will get a sexually transmitted disease today—and most of them will marry somebody one day. Many STDs are treatable but incurable, and most will share the disease with their future spouses.

There are also emotional considerations that can affect your marriage for ten or more years. What you do tonight can still be bothering you—and others—ten years from now. Often marriage counselors must help spouses deal with their guilt over premarital sexual partners before they can help them have a healthy sexual relationship within marriage. Many marriages are sexually dysfunctional because of the guilt and resentment that come as baggage from previous relationships. When old boyfriends or girlfriends are introduced, what goes through your new spouse's mind? Why not plan now to give your future partner the one gift that you can give only once—and don't let him or her open it until the wedding night.

Look past the present to the future. There will come a time in the not-too-distant future when you will be very pleased to look your son in the eye and say, "Son, I'm thirty-five years old and I've never tasted alcohol in my life. If I could resist it, you can, too." You'll be able to have a heart-to-heart with your daughter and say, "Honey, your dad and I want you to save yourself for marriage. We were virgins on our wedding night and it was wonderful! We want that for you, too."

The final grade

Ask Eve about sin as she is escorted from Paradise with no return ticket. That slippery snake said nothing about this "graduation" from Sin's School. Don't hang this diploma on your wall!

Discussion Questions

1. What are some dangers of leaving God in the teen years, with the intent of returning to Him later in life?

2. What is a good way to handle someone who pressures you to participate in his or her sins?

3. After eating the fruit, what things did Adam and Eve know that they did not know before? Did the devil tell the truth when he said that they would be "like God"?

4. Read Proverbs 20:1 and 23:29–35 and discuss some of the consequences of drinking alcohol.

5. What would you say to a friend who says that none of these bad consequences will happen to him?

6. What are some possible negative consequences of sexual activity before marriage?

CHAPTER

2

The Far Country Will Take You Farther Than You Want to Go

Lesson text: Jonah 1–2

Memory verse: "Then when lust hath conceived, it bringeth forth sin: and sin, when it is finished, bringeth forth death" (James 1:15).

When Christian teens decide to experiment with sin, they adopt a "sin now; repent later" philosophy. They usually don't intend to leave God forever. When they get older, they plan to come back.

They don't think about the dangers of the far country. They don't realize that it will take them farther than they want to go. Coming home may be harder than they think.

If Luke 15 had listed the prodigal boy's itinerary for his trip to the far country, it might have included "beaches, bars, and brothels." But he had to read the very fine print to find "pig farm." His "summer trip" took him farther than he intended to go. Once you board sin's train, it can be awfully hard to disembark.

Ask Jonah.

God told Jonah to go east to preach in Nineveh, the capital of the

Assyrian Empire (Jonah 1:1–2). Jonah went west to hide in Tarshish, a city in southwest Spain (1:3). When he got on that boat, he had no idea how far sin was going to take him. God sent a storm and nearly sank the ship. The mariners discovered that Jonah was running from God and threw him overboard.

Stop and think.

What was that like? Jonah described it: "For thou hadst cast me into the deep, in the midst of the seas; and the floods compassed me about: all thy billows and thy waves passed over me" (Jonah 2:3). Drowning is a horrible way to die; to nearly drown is one of the most frightening experiences one can have. Why is Jonah in the water? Sin has taken him farther than he wanted to go.

Instead of allowing him to drown, though, the Lord sent a great fish to swallow Jonah (Jonah 1:17). Imagine what it felt like to be swallowed by a fish! Why are you in the fish, Jonah? Sin.

Down he went to the sea bottom (Jonah 2:6). Why are you there, Jonah? Sin. For three days Jonah was in a fish's digestive system! What did it smell like? What did it feel like? "The waters compassed me about, even to the soul: the depth closed me round about, the weeds were wrapped about my head" (Jonah 2:5).

Finally, God decided class was over and had the fish vomit (God's word, not mine, *qow'*, "to spue out; vomit out, up, up again, 2:10) Jonah out onto land. What did it feel like to be human vomit? What made Jonah the only person to ever find out? Sin.

What did Jonah learn? Sin will take you farther than you want to go.

What does Jonah teach us about taking a trip into sin?

It's easy to book passage

Jonah didn't have to wait for a ship going to Tarshish—the devil had it ready for him (Jonah 1:3). Satan keeps "boats at the dock" for anybody wanting to sail to "Tarshish" (cf. 2 Corinthians 2:11). The devil is always on the prowl

(1 Peter 5:8). Sin always lies "at the door" (Genesis 4:7). It is a wide gate that leads to the broad road (Matthew 7:13). If you remain true to God, it won't be because you lacked opportunities to sin; it will be because you had the backbone to say no to sin and the faith to say yes to God.

What "boats" does Satan keep ready?

- As teens heading to "Tarshish," we find that being underage is no real hindrance to buying beer or cigarettes—an older friend will get it for us, or an unscrupulous business man will sell it to us "under the table" (cf. Proverbs 1:19).

- If we want to tell dirty jokes, there are plenty of people who will laugh. Many people take pleasure in sin (cf. Romans 1:32).

- If we want to go places and do things our parents forbid, we find that friends will lie to our parents for us (cf. Ephesians 6:1–2; 2 Timothy 3:2).

- If we want to do drugs, it is not hard to find someone who can get whatever we want—for a price. It's so easy to find drugs that about twenty-five teens start using every hour of every day of every year in America (that's 500 per day; 182,500 per year). These substances take control of the mind and body, in violation of Paul's command: "Neither yield ye your members as instruments of unrighteousness unto sin: but yield yourselves unto God, as those that are alive from the dead, and your members as instruments of righteousness unto God" (Romans 6:13).

- If we want to start a sexual relationship, most don't have to look far to find a willing partner. Solomon warned his son that there were women who were on the lookout for sexual partners (Proverbs 9:14–17). If the truth were told, some young men ask girls on dates only for the purpose of sexual fulfillment.

U-Turns and exits are hard to find

Sin is progressive. It's a slide on a slippery slope that goes down, down, down. The road into the "far country" is always downhill. Jonah went "down" to Joppa, "down" into the ship (Jonah 1:3), "down" into the sea, "down" into the fish's mouth, and "down" to the sea bottom. By contrast, it is a "highway" of holiness that leads to God (Isaiah 35:8).

Think of sin's downward progression:

- Walking with the ungodly leads to standing with sinners; standing with sinners leads to sitting with the scornful (Psalm 1:1; Matthew 26:58, 69–75).

- Anger leads to violence; wrath leads to hatred; hatred leads to murder (Genesis 4:6, 8; Proverbs 27:3; Daniel 2:12; 1 John 3:15).

- Jealousy and envy lead to cruelty, slander, and vengeance (Proverbs 6:34; 27:4; Song of Solomon 8:6; Judges 19:29–30).

- Disobedience to parents leads to lying to parents (Romans 1:30; Ephesians 4:15; cf. Genesis 26:7; Colossians 3:9).

- One lie leads to more lies (cf. John 8:44).

- Covetousness leads to stealing and stealing to violence (Joshua 7:21; 1 Kings 21:1–15; Micah 2:1–2; Mark 7:22; Ephesians 4:28; 2 Peter 2:3).

- R-rated movies lead to X-rated movies; soft-core porn leads to hard-core (Matthew 5:28; 1 Peter 2:11); pornography often leads to rape and child molestation. Eighty teens are raped every day in America, and 3,610 are assaulted.

- Immodest clothes, dancing, and petting lead to lust, and lust leads to fornication (Matthew 5:28; Galatians 5:19–21; 2 Timothy 2:22).

- Perverted thoughts lead to homosexuality (Romans 1:26–27; cf. Genesis 19:5; Leviticus 18:22; Judges 19:22; 1 Corinthians 6:9; 1 Timothy 1:10; Jude 1:7, 10); homosexuality can lead to pedophilia (child rape/molestation).

- Smoking cigarettes often leads to smoking marijuana (1 Corinthians 6:19–20); smoking marijuana leads to harder drugs (Romans 6:13). Five hundred adolescents began using drugs today—every day, and many of them began with cigarettes and marijuana.

The road is full of curves, holes, and bumps

A sinful life is a turbulent life. Jonah found himself in a storm. It usually doesn't take long for teens who forsake Christ to find turmoil (Proverbs 4:19; 15:10; Jeremiah 2:19; Romans 6:21).

Eli's sons found no escape from sin. Ultimately, they were slain (1 Samuel 4:11). Sin is no plaything. First we toy with sin, and then sin toys with us. To begin with, we play master, and it plays slave; then we switch, and sin doesn't want to take turns anymore. James said, "Then when lust hath conceived, it bringeth forth sin: and sin, when it is finished, bringeth forth death" (James 1:15).

One rancher posted on his gates and fences a sign to stop trespassers on his property.

STOP. I know you're thinking about crossing this gate. What you should know is that if the Coyotes, Cactus, Mesquite, Heat, Dust, or Rattlers don't get you, my Winchester will.

If sin's immediate consequences don't get us, eventually God's Judgment Day will.

Discussion Questions

1. How hard is it to find a source for drugs, cigarettes, or alcohol at your school or in your community? What tactics do you use to avoid these temptations?

2. If someone wants to tell you a dirty joke, how do you handle it?

3. What Bible verse would forbid taking drugs?

4. Give some examples of how one sin leads to another sin, and often a "minor" sin leads to a "major" sin (in terms of consequences).

5. How is homosexuality viewed among your friends? Has God's view changed?

The Far Country Will Keep You Longer Than You Want to Stay

Lesson text: 2 Samuel 11:1–5 and 12:1–10

Memory verse: "But every man is tempted, when he is drawn away of his own lust, and enticed" (James 1:14).

T he boy in Jesus' story is the exception. The truth is, most prodigals never come home. Oh, they think they will. They plan to . . . some-day. They may even start back toward home . . . several times. But it's a long way back. It's embarrassing to admit you've been wrong. Sin's entanglements are confusing to unravel. Bad habits are hard to break; bad friends are difficult to give up; bad reputations are hard to live down.

You don't believe the "most" part? Flip through an old church directory with an older member of the congregation you attend. Look at the faces of the young people about your age from a few years ago. Ask, "Where is he now? Is she still 'in church?' Are their children in Bible classes?" In many cases, the answers will be, "Yes." These are usually the ones who stayed "at the father's house." Oh, they were not perfect in their teen years. They had to repent, confess sin, and start again—perhaps several times. But they stayed with it.

"What about the others?" you ask. The prodigals, the ones who experimented, exposed, and enjoyed the "pleasures of sin for a season" (Hebrews 11:25). A few of them are happy endings. They came to themselves and came home.

The others? Well, they married one of the girls or guys from the far country. Somebody they met at a party or a bar. Somebody they "experimented with." Somebody that never knew the Lord and doesn't care much about knowing Him now (cf. 1 Samuel 2:12; 3:7). On Sundays they prefer the lake to the Lord. When it comes to reading, they prefer the day's news to the Good News. They still drink a little (on the weekends), still smoke (a pack a day now), still use bad language (when they are with the guys or in a foul mood), still watch bad movies, and—well, you get the picture. They're still in the pigpen. It's hard to leave.

From a "peeping tom" to a "weeping king"

Ask David.

His sin started as a Peeping Tom watching his next door neighbor take her bath (2 Samuel 11:2). He looked (she was beautiful), lusted (she was naked), sent for (it's hard to say no to a king), and slept with her (11:4). That was about as long as he had planned to stay in the far country—a one night excursion. Most kings of that day just took any woman they wanted for a wife into their harem, but David sent her back home (11:4). What David was about to find out was that although he was through with sin, sin wasn't through with him.

A few weeks later an unwelcome note was passed to him. It must have been tightly sealed with *King's Eyes Only* on the envelope. It was probably spotted and smeared with tears. He opened it to read the four words he must have secretly dreaded ever since another man's wife got out of his bed: "I am with child" (2 Samuel 11:5).

He was back on board the sin train—and it was going to keep him much longer than he wanted to stay. You know the downward spiral his life took from there. Deception. Hypocrisy. Conniving. Dishonor. Murder. Cover-up. Quickie Marriage (2 Samuel 11:6–27).

Ask David.

The next scene is God's prophet paying the former shepherd a visit with a parable about a rich man, a poor man, and a pet lamb (2 Samuel 12:1–5). The poor man loved his pet lamb like it was his own child. He had kept it a long time. It ate at his table. The rich man killed it . . . to feed to a passing guest.

Perhaps David, who thought this was a true story, thought of a pet lamb he had growing up. His face flushed with anger, and he rendered this judicial decision: "He shall pay back fourfold" (12:6). Unwittingly, David had just pronounced his own sentence and rewritten the script for the last two decades of his life. The rest of David's years read like a plot out of daytime television. Sin was about to take him for a long ride.

- Ask David how far sin will take you as he lies for a week in the dirt praying for a dying baby.

- Ask him at 3:00 A.M. on the seventh day when he hasn't slept or eaten (2 Samuel 12:16–19).

- Ask him again as he walks home from the burial (12:19).

- Ask him again later when he learns that his daughter has just been raped—while on an errand on which he sent her (2 Samuel 13:12–14).

- Ask him again when he finds out that one of his sons is the rapist. Put yourself in this father's place "when king David heard of all these things" (13:21).

- Ask him again when the message comes that his son had just been murdered—because David had sent him into harm's way.

- Ask him again when he finds out that another son is the murderer (2 Samuel 13:30–32).

- Ask him again when he doesn't see his own son's face for five years (2 Samuel 13:38; 14:24–32).

- Ask him again as he flees his palace one night, barefoot and weeping, because that son is trying to kill him and take his kingdom (2 Samuel 15:30).

- Ask him again as he ducks flying rocks and flinches from cursing insults (2 Samuel 16:13).

- Ask him again when he—along with all Israel—hears that his son has slept with ten of David's wives (concubines are "secondary or lesser wives") in a tent on top of the king's palace (2 Samuel 16:22). David had done his sin in secret; this embarrassment was known "in the sight of all Israel."

- Ask him again when his close friend betrays him and wants an opportunity to murder him (2 Samuel 17:1–2).

- Ask again between his sobs as he grieves that his beloved son is swinging from an oak by his hair with three darts through his heart (2 Samuel 18:14, 33).

Sin took David farther than he ever wanted to go.
How far is sin taking teens today?

- Have you witnessed the anger, sadness, depression, hatefulness, and hopelessness of a life Satan gives back after an extended stay in the far country?

- Have you looked into the vacant eyes of a young person who has been living a worldly lifestyle for several months?

- Have you been around the miserable pessimist who has lost faith in God and the Bible?

- Have you seen a youth robbed of innocence and purity?

- Have you sat with a teen who cries until she or he runs out of tears, because the consequences of sin have become personal instead of theoretical?

- Have you been to rehab with a young person whose body has the shakes of withdrawal, the hollow eyes, the bloodless face, the wasted body?

- Have you attended the funeral of a teen whom sin took so far that he decided death by bullet or pills was better than life? On average, a teen takes his or her own life every four hours in this country.

Bad habits will keep you longer than you want to stay

Sin is addictive. And it's not just the obvious ones—drugs, alcohol, smoking, gambling—all sin is habit-forming.

Lying is addictive. Once a person becomes a liar, a lie will come easier to his lips than the truth. He will tell a lie when the truth would have served him better (Proverbs 8:7; John 8:44; Acts 5:3–4; Ephesians 4:25; Colossians 3:9; 1 Timothy 1:10; 4:2; Titus 1:2, 12; Revelation 21:8; 22:15).

Cursing is addictive. There are men, and some women, who curse without even thinking about it. They can hardly open their mouths without using God's name in vain. Even when they try to stop, they can hardly keep the words from slipping out (Psalm 10:7; 59:12; 109:17–18; James 3:10).

Sex sin is addictive. Because there is pleasure in sex sin (Hebrews 11:25), once one starts, it is very hard to stop (cf. 1 Corinthians 6:15–20; Matthew 5:27–28; Galatians 5:19–21). Don't think marriage will remove the temptation, either. One who sleeps around before marriage will find it hard not to run around on his wife (her husband) after marriage (Proverbs 5:20–23).

Cheating is addictive (cf. Romans 12:17). Some students work harder trying to cheat than they would have had to work to read the material and answer the questions. Once one starts cheating, it is hard to go back to studying for honest grades.

Gluttony is addictive (Proverbs 23:21; Philippians 3:19). It is easy to become addicted to overeating for two reasons: food tastes good, and it is usually available in abundance. Overeating is a sin many Christians commit regularly without even recognizing the sin involved, which is a lack of self-control (Acts 24:25; Galatians 5:23; 2 Peter 1:6).

Immodest dress is addictive. It is surprisingly hard to go back to styles that are "right" when one is used to "slight and tight" (1 Timothy 2:9; cf. Mark 5:15). It is ironic that a young lady returning from the far country of fashion feels more self-conscious with clothes that properly cover than she does with those that should make her feel self-conscious (cf. Jeremiah 6:15).

Smoking is addictive. To many teens, it seems "cool" to sneak a few cigarettes and "cough" their way through them. Twenty-thousand packs later (a pack a day for fifty years), one is hacking his way through the final stages of a life prematurely ended due to nicotine-inflicted injury (cf. 1 Corinthians 6:19–20).

At a gospel meeting in Tennessee a few years ago, I preached part of a sermon on why Christians should not harm their bodies by smoking. When the service ended, a man wearing an oxygen mask and pulling a tank behind him (because smoking had ruined his lungs) walked up to me. I was afraid he had been offended and might "let off a little steam in the preacher's ear." To the contrary, this Christian gentleman said, "Son, please don't stop preaching about smoking. I've quit, but it's too late for me. I wish someone had told me what you said tonight when I was young."

Young people, I know a lot of adults who smoke, but I do not know a single one who doesn't wish he or she had never started. Smoking is a habit that will keep you longer than you want to stay.

Bad company will keep you longer than you want to stay

Almost every parent and teen has had a conversation on this subject. The Bible often warns against bad companions, too. Regardless of what people say, it is still true that leaven leavens the lump (1 Corinthians 5:6; 15:33). He who lies with dogs will rise with fleas. Like the flour miller who left a little flour on all those he brushed against on the way home from work, so we leave a deposit of our personality on all of those with whom we associate each day.

Bad groups can be hard to leave. I recently counseled a gang member who was trying to get out of his gang. He wanted to get his life back on the right track. He explained, "They won't let you get out— they say, 'the only way out is death.'" He was running scared because they had been trying to shoot him.

Fraternities and sororities are often like this, too. Don't join a wild fraternity or sorority when you get to college. Sadly, their reputation for drinking and wild, ungodly behavior is well-earned (some professional clubs do not fit in this category). And once you know their secrets (handshakes, rituals, passwords), they won't let you out. No, they won't put a price on your head or try to take you out in a drive-by shooting, but they will blackball you. That is, you'll be immediately socially ostracized, and, after you graduate to the business world, they network against you. That means that they try to keep you from getting a job, receiving promotions, and joining in their professional circles.

Think of the time lost in the far country of sin. For David it was about nine months. (Nathan the prophet evidently came just before the baby was born). Wasted time . . . days given to the devil. But this is nothing compared to what many young people do. They give Satan *years*. They leave God at sixteen, not to return until they are thirty . . . or forty . . . or . . . seventy— perhaps never.

Solomon said, "Remember now thy Creator in the days of thy youth, while the evil days come not, nor the years draw nigh, when thou shalt say, I have no pleasure in them" (Ecclesiastes 12:1). Paul told us to redeem the time, because the days are evil (Ephesians 5:16). This seems to mean that hard times are coming, so you better use the easy times to get ready. Don't give the devil your young mind and body.

There will come a time when you cannot remember as you can now; learning God's Word and memorizing Scriptures will be much harder. There will come a time when you will wish you could sing God a beautiful song, but your voice will be old and cracked. There will come a day when you will wish that you could go to worship services just one more time, but your health will not allow it. There will come a day when you will wish you could work for God, but your body will have lost its strength. Use the opportunities that God gives today so you won't have to live with regrets tomorrow.

How sad that many can sing from personal experience, "Years I spent in vanity and pride, caring not my Lord was crucified." The far country will keep you longer than you want to stay—maybe even for eternity.

Discussion Questions

1. Why is it hard to leave the "pigpen" of sin?

2. Retell the parable that Nathan told David and explain what it meant.

3. What are some of the bad things that happened to David after he let sin enter his life?

4. What are some sins that are addictive to young people today?

5. What does the Bible mean when it says, "A little leaven leaveneth the whole lump"? (1 Corinthians 5:6).

6. Explain in your own words what 1 Corinthians 15:33 means. Use examples (not someone in the room, or known to those in the room).

7. How wise is it to give the devil the best years of one's life, and then give God the "left over" years?

8. Imagine yourself twenty years from now explaining to your children what kind of friends they should choose. What would you say?

The Far Country Will Cost You More Than You Want to Pay

Lesson text: Judges 14–16

Memory verse: "For the wages of sin is death; but the gift of God is eternal life through Jesus Christ our Lord" (Romans 6:23).

The word *prodigal* doesn't mean "wild." It means "wasteful." The prodigal son "wasted his substance with rioteous living" (Luke 15:13). And you know what? He never got it back. Sure, he got a "welcome home bar-be-cue" (fatted calf), a change of clothes (the best robe and shoes), and some jewelry (a ring) when he came home. But he didn't get his inheritance back. When his father went out to talk to his older brother, he told that son, "All that I have is thine." The Father would not divide again his possessions and give the younger son another inheritance. There was a price to pay for going to the far country.

Ask Samson.

The High Price Samson Paid for a Good Time

Samson would have fit in pretty well in our world. Big, strong guy. He would have probably been the captain of the football team. Must have been good looking, too. He always had a girl on his arm (Judges 14:1, 7; 16:1). Liked to have a good time. A jokester—bet on riddles (Judges 14:12), got into fights (Judges 15:8), toyed with sin in Delilah's lap.

Way to go Samson, some would say. Well, there is more to the story— the cost-you-more-than-you-want-to-pay part. Samson played with fire until he got burnt. He was the strongest man who ever lived, yet he was also one of the weakest. He fell for a woman named Delilah, whom the Philistines hired to find the secret of his great strength. He got his kicks from "high stakes" gambling with her—he literally played a game of life and death (Judges 16:6). He teased her by telling her "secrets," only to laugh when she believed him and brought in Philistines to overpower him (Judges 16:7–15). She finally got the last laugh, though. She worried him until he gave in—and gave out his secret: "If my hair is cut, my strength will be gone."

She got him to fall asleep on her knees, and while he slept, she had his hair cut off (Judges 16:19). Then she turned him over to the Philistines who put out his eyes. (Imagine that! Judges 16:21), and forced him to do hard slave labor. They brought him before large crowds to mock him (Judges 16:25). Ultimately, Samson lay dead under a pile of rubble that had been a Philistine building (Judges 16:30). Samson played with sin; then sin played with Samson. It had cost him more than he wanted to pay.

Sin comes with an expensive price tag today, too. It has wages—but instead of getting them, you have to pay them (Romans 6:21, 23). Yes, sin often costs money. A rock of crack is about $20; an "eight ball" (3.45 mg) of cocaine is $150; a gram of meth is $100; a marijuana joint is $10; a six-pack of beer is about $6.00; a pack of cigs is about $4.00; a dirty magazine is $5.00.

Sin, however, costs much more than money. The numbers above were supplied by Officer Kevin Briley of the Anniston, Alabama, Police Department, in consultation with the narcotics division. He adds this note about the cost of drugs: "Also keep in mind the cost if you get caught and go to court. I think court costs are around $100, plus the fine set by the judge. Plus any kind of rehab or counseling that the judge may order has to be paid for the person going. Also the loss of a driver's license that may get suspended if you were in a car, [and] you have to pay to get it reinstated. The car will probably get towed. Towing fees are about $75 for the tow and $10–$15 per day storage fee. Not to mention jail or prison, and the pain that one's family goes through. A lot of times a drug user will steal from his or her family to sell things or trade them for drugs. They steal from the family because generally it will take the family longer to press charges against a family member."

What did sin cost Samson?

Sin cost Samson his eyes

Imagine asking Samson, "Would you trade your eyes for a relationship with a pretty Philistine?" He would have looked at you like you were crazy. But after his time with Delilah, he couldn't look at you at all. How does this relate to us? Sin blinds the sinner. A rabbit that turns to look at oncoming headlights usually ends up dead. A Christian who turns to face the devil finds the same consequence (2 Corinthians 4:3–4; Revelation 3:17–18; 2 Peter 1:5–11; 1 John 2:9, 11; Matthew 13:15; Ephesians 4:18).

Sin cost Samson his freedom

"Samson, would you be willing to go to jail for Delilah?" He would have quickly replied, "She's not worth that!" Yet that is what it cost him. What's the point? Sin enslaves (John 8:34; Romans 6:16–20; 2 Peter 2:19; Proverbs 5:22).

When asked about drinking, smoking, drugs, or gambling, a young person might say, "I can take it or leave it," meaning that they do it but are not addicted. You can mark it down—they are taking it! Before long, sin will enslave them, and when the devil says "jump," they will only ask, "How high?"

Sin cost Samson his strength

Ask almost any child who goes to Bible class, "Who is the strong man in the Bible?" He will tell you, "Samson." He is one of the most famous men who ever lived—a well-known character even to people who don't read the Bible.

The pagans took the historical Samson and invented the mythological Hercules. Samson delighted in his muscles. He often showed off what he could do . . . killed a lion with his bare hands (Judges 14:5–6) . . . took a donkey's jawbone and killed a thousand soldiers (Judges 15:16) . . . ripped Gaza's city gate doors out of the wall and carried them sixteen miles to Hebron and left the citizens to figure a way to get them back (Judges 16:3) . . . let people tie him up so he could snap the ropes (Judges 15:13–14; 16:7–9).

Imagine asking, "Samson, what would you take in exchange for your strength?" He would have answered, "Nothing!"

Nonetheless, toying with sin left him as weak as any other man (Judges 16:17). God wants strong young people (Ephesians 6:10; 1 Corinthians 16:13; 2 Timothy 2:1; Colossians 1:11), but sin always weakens us (1 Corinthians 11:30). Sin will weaken one spiritually (it's easier to give in to temptation the second time, and even easier the third), physically (many good athletes have let drinking, drugs, and smoking ruin their chances for scholarships and pro careers), and emotionally (less stable, less "in control" of themselves).

Sin cost Samson his honor (Judges 16:25)

It's hard to know what to think of Samson. He is an interesting character—plenty of sermons have been preached about him. But when someone makes a list of favorite Old Testament characters, Samson rarely makes the cut. Abraham, Isaac, Jacob, Joseph, Moses, David, Solomon, Elijah, but not Samson.

And it's not just modern people. He receives only one passing reference in the entire rest of the Bible (Hebrews 11:32). Sin cost him his dignity. Eventually, it always does. Think back to Eve, David, and Jonah. Eve tried to hide from her sin; David tried to cover his, and Jonah . . . well, I wonder how much he thought of himself in that fish's belly or when he was vomited onto the shore, covered with fish slime and seaweed?

Sin disgraces us, too. Sin can keep us from looking others in the eye, or even liking the person we look at in the mirror. The ungodly will not be able to hold up their heads in the judgment (Psalm 1:5). They ultimately face "everlasting shame and contempt" (Daniel 12:2).

What others think of us is not as important as what God thinks of us, but it is important. Good influence is one of a Christian's most valuable treasures. It is to be guarded even at great cost. Nehemiah said in the long ago: "Ought ye not to walk in the fear of our God because of the reproach of the heathen our enemies?" (Nehemiah 5:9).

The Christian's light must never lose its sparkle; her salt must never lose its flavor (Matthew 5:14–16); his leaven must never lose its power (Matthew 13:33). He must use "sound speech, that cannot be condemned; that he that is of the contrary part may be ashamed, having no evil thing to say" (Titus 2:8). She should "give none occasion to the adversary to speak reproachfully" (1 Timothy 5:14). He should have his "conversation honest among the Gentiles: that, whereas they speak against you as evildoers, they may by your good works, which they shall behold, glorify God in the day of visitation" (1 Peter 2:12; cf. 2:15; 3:16).

Don't let sin steal your honor, and thus your influence. Let vigilance keep her constant watch lest sin steal our power to lead others to Christ.

Sin cost Samson his companions

Samson enjoyed people—especially women. Yet when sin was done with him, he sat in a lonely Gaza prison cell. Sin and separation go together. Sin often leaves us lonely. It separates us from our God (Isaiah 59:1–2), our families (Genesis 19), our self-respect (Galatians 5:17–23; Romans 7:18–25), our Christian friends (2 Thessalonians 3:6), and often from our worldly friends. How many friends would you guess the prodigal had in the pigpen?

Sin cost Samson his life

"Samson, how long do you want to live?"

"A long time. I want to die an old man. I want to see my children grow up and enjoy my grandchildren," he would have replied. How did it turn out? Samson died young—probably at about forty. He judged Israel twenty years (Judges 16:31), and seems to have started judging when he was in his late teens—still at his father's house. Most other Bible characters lived longer. Why the shortened pilgrimage? Sin cost him more than he wanted to pay.

Sin brings death today, too. "The soul that sinneth, it shall die" (Ezekiel 18:20). "The wages of sin is death" (Romans 6:23). In the end sin always "brings forth death" (James 1:15), since all unforgiven sinners will experience the second death (Revelation 21:8).

Like Balaam, Samson's affections were often divided between doing what was right and doing what he wanted (Numbers 22:13–20, 37–38; 24:13–14; 31:16; Judges 13–16). Like King Saul of Israel, Samson had a promising beginning but a tragic end (1 Samuel 9:21; 15:30–35; Judges 13:24–25; 16:21–30). Like Solomon, his love of foreign women ultimately destroyed him (1 Kings 11:1–3; Judges 14:1–3; 16:1–21).

Forgiveness from sin is wonderful. Yet forgiveness of the guilt of sin is different from freedom from the consequences of sin. We all live downstream from sin's consequences. David repented of his sin with Bathsheba (Psalm 51), but the sword never departed from his house (2 Samuel 12:10–13). Esau repented of selling his birthright, and sought it again with tears, but was unable to retrieve it (Hebrews 12:16–17).

Sins still have consequences today. You might throw that pack of cigarettes away, but you will have to fight desperately not to stop at the convenience store on the way home to buy another one. You might repent of doing drugs, but your body will still crave a fix. You might throw your porno movies away, but you'll never go into another video store without wanting to peruse the "mature aisle." You may repent of having sex with your girlfriend, but that will not make either of you sexually pure again—or perhaps make her any less pregnant. You might repent of drinking, but that will not bring back the guy that got killed in the car wreck.

Note: The four main points (chapter titles) are not original, nor are all the "Samson" sub-points. Many preachers have used them through the years. If you know an original source, please let us know so we can give proper credit.

Discussion Questions

1. What does the word "prodigal" mean?

2. When the prodigal son returned home, what did he get back? What did he not get back?

3. When a sinner comes back to God, what does he (she) get back? What does he (she) not get back?

4. What are some of Samson's amazing physical feats?

5. Describe how Samson toyed with sin.

6. What was the secret of Samson's strength? How did Delilah get the last laugh at Samson's expense?

7. Explain what is meant by, "Samson played with fire until he got burnt."

8. Do you agree with the statement: "Good influence is one of a Christian's most valuable treasures"? Explain.

CHAPTER

5

The Weaknesses of
a Strong Man

Lesson text: Judges 14–16

Memory verse: "I can do all things through Christ which strengtheneth me" (Philippians 4:13).

Samson is called the strongest man in the Bible. He once carried the doors of a city gate sixteen miles (Judges 16:3). He killed a thousand men with nothing more than a donkey's jawbone (Judges 15:15–17). He tore a lion apart with his bare hands (Judges 14:5–6). He demolished a coliseum (Judges 16:30).

As strong as he was, he would also be in the running for the weakest man in the Bible.

As strong as Samson was, he was not strong enough to overcome bad companions

The statement, "Samson went down" (Judges 14:1) is true both geographically and spiritually. We begin here to notice the reckless attitude that dominated his adult years. Instead of staying within Israel's borders, he went into enemy territory to find friends. He deliberately chose evil associations—the woman of

Timnath, a harlot in Gaza, and Delilah of Sorek (Judges 14:1–7; 16:1–20; cf. Proverbs 1:10–15; 4:14)—and these relationships eventually destroyed him.

As Christians, we should not see how close we can come to evil and not be tainted. The words "put off" in Colossians 3:8 mean, "to move out of and away from." As Israel had to get out of Egypt and then move away from its borders, so Christians leaving worldliness must put some distance between it and themselves. We should be careful about our associates for four reasons.

(1) We will be judged by those with whom we associate. Most people know the old saying is true, "Birds of a feather flock together." We tend to gravitate to people who are most like us (cf. Amos 3:3). The Bible teaches that Christians are the "salt of the earth," "light of the world," and "a city which is set on a hill" (Matthew 5:13–14). As such, Christians cannot be friends of the world (James 4:4), in fellowship with the unfruitful works of darkness (Ephesians 5:11), or be a servant of both God and mammon (Matthew 6:24).

(2) We will choose a companion from among our associates. Samson fell in love with a heathen woman. Should an Israelite—especially a Nazarite, who was totally devoted to the Lord—desire to become one flesh with a worshipper of Dagon? Samson knew the laws of separation God had given to the Jews, but he chose to ignore them (Exodus 34:16; Deuteronomy 7:1–3; cf. Genesis 6:2; 24:3–4; 26:34–35). Why did he choose the woman of Timnath? He does not say that he found her to be wise, spiritually strong, or virtuous. Rather, his sole criteria for choosing his marriage partner was summed up in, "She pleaseth me well" (Judges 14:3), which means "She is right in mine eyes." It was a physical attraction.

His parents wisely tried to dissuade him from yoking himself unequally with an unbeliever (2 Corinthians 6:14), but he defied them (cf. Ephesians 6:1–3). He told them; he did not ask them. "Get her for me," he insisted, "for she pleases me well!" In those days, parents arranged marriages, and there were several months between the engagement and the wedding. (How embarrassed his parents must have been to go to their enemies and ask for this girl.) God wants His children to marry His children (Matthew 6:33; Luke 2:51; 1 Corinthians 9:5; 2 Corinthians 6:14–18).

While it is true that every marriage is a mixed marriage—a mixture of personalities, social backgrounds, dreams, and aspirations—a wise person does not willingly add the conflict of religious mixture. By doing so, he places his most valuable asset, his soul, on the gambler's table (Matthew 16:26). An old man wisely said, "If a Christian marries a child of the devil, he is going to have a lot of trouble with his father-in-law." Many have doubted it in their youth, pondered it in their maturity, and will regret it in their eternity.

(3) We become like those with whom we associate. Leaven leavens the lump (1 Corinthians 5:6; 15:33). While perhaps not politically correct, two old sayings have a point: "He who lies with a cripple learns to limp"; and, "He who lies down with dogs will rise up with fleas."

(4) They will lead to our fall. Many strong men have fallen through bad associations. Samson did. Solomon did (1 Kings 11). Peter denied the Lord while warming at Satan's fire (Mark 14:66–72). What is at stake when we choose our friends? Heaven or hell may well turn out to be the answer.

As strong as Samson was, he was not strong enough to control his emotions

Samson could set the Philistine fields on fire, but he could not control the fire of his own lust. He killed a lion, but he could not put to death the anger of his heart. He could kill a thousand men, but he could not stand up to his own feelings. He could easily break the cords that men put on his hands, but sin's shackles gradually imprisoned his soul.

A Nazarite volunteered to live for God, but Samson chose to live for himself. Lust, anger, revenge, and hatred directed Samson's actions. His great failure was a lack of self-control (cf. Ephesians 4:27; Acts 24:25; Galatians 5:23; Colossians 3:2–10; 2 Peter 1:6). Similarly, how tragic it is when God gives one a wonderful heritage and great opportunities, and he or she treats them lightly.

Anger. Samson reminds us of Solomon's proverb: "He that is slow to anger is better than the mighty; and he that ruleth his spirit than he that taketh a city" (Proverbs 16:32). Samson challenged those attending the wedding feast to solve a riddle. They wagered thirty garments, which was an expensive bet at that time. When the Philistines could not figure out the answer, they pressured Samson's new wife to get it for them. It was unscrupulous to ask her to betray her own husband. As a wife, she was to forget her own people (cf. Ruth 1:14–17; Psalm 45:10). Nonetheless, she did as they requested.

Samson could not bear to have his love questioned, and after her tears he finally told her the riddle. She quickly told his enemies. Angered by her betrayal, Samson went to Ashkelon and killed thirty men and gave their garments to his competitor. Still angry, Samson failed to consummate the marriage and stormed back to his parents' house.

Revenge. After some months, Samson's anger cooled and he went back to take his wife—only to discover that she had been given to his best man! Samson became so vengeful that he began a one-man war with the Philistines. One thing led to another. He burned their fields; they burned his wife's family's house—with them in it! (Judges 14:15; 15:4–6). Samson avenged their death with a ruthless slaughter of Philistine soldiers.

After he retired to Etam, three thousand Israelites turned him over to his enemies (Judges 15:11–13). As Samson was being delivered to the Philistines, he broke the ropes, and with the jawbone of a donkey killed one thousand Philistine warriors.

Like Samson, we may want to avenge a wrong and get even with those who embarrassed or cheated us. Instead, God wants us to avoid seeking revenge (Romans 12:17–19) and turn the other cheek (Matthew 5:39).

Lust. Samson had already gotten into serious trouble with one woman, but his lust lead him to Philistia again, where he visited a harlot in Gaza (Judges 16:1–3). His enemies found out and made plans to ambush Samson the next morning, but he left during the night, carrying the doors of the city gate some sixteen miles to Hebron!

Serving God involves not just separating from something; it is also includes separating to something. We must separate from worldly lusts (Matthew 5:28); we must separate to positive service to God and others (Philippians 2:3–4).

As strong as Samson was, he was not strong enough to overcome Satan's temptations

The devil must be resisted (James 4:7). Samson did not resist strongly enough, so he compromised his convictions. The vow of the Nazarite included three restrictions:

- Abstinence from strong drink (alcohol);
- Hair left uncut during the time of the vow;
- No contact with a dead body.

It was essentially a vow to abstain from fleshly lusts (1 Peter 2:11). He was not to yield his members to evil (Romans 6:13); he was to attain self-control. From that discipline his body and soul would derive strength.

Samson allowed himself to be prodded until he became disloyal to his vow. Although we have no record of him partaking of alcohol or touching a dead body, unless you count the lion or those on the battlefield, we do know that he broke the stipulation about not cutting his hair. James says, "For whosoever shall keep the whole law, and yet offend in one point, he is guilty of all" (James 2:10). This does not mean that if we break one commandment we might as well go ahead and break them all. It is teaching that the attitude that leads one to disobey God one time will lead one to break God's law many times, if the circumstances call for it. One does not have to break every civil law to be a criminal; he only has to be convicted of breaking one law.

Samson gave in. As he had given in to the woman of Timnath and told her the riddle after seven days (Judges 14:17), he gave in to Delilah and revealed the secret of his strength (Judges 16:16–17). By contrast, Joseph never gave in (Genesis 39:8–13); Vashti never gave in (Esther 1:1–22); Shadrach, Meshech, and Abednego never gave in (Daniel 3:12–30). A half-hearted commitment will not last long. Many today have stood for a short time but finally succumbed to their friend's taunts. By giving in, young people have renounced their convictions, lost their virtue, and forfeited their souls.

The world's strongest man was a weakling. Don't be like him.

Discussion Questions

1. Explain the difference between forgiveness of the guilt of sin and freedom from the consequences of sin. Give examples.

2. Why is Samson called both the strongest man of the Bible and one of the weakest men of the Bible?

3. Is the way someone looks the only criteria for choosing a boyfriend or girlfriend? When one considers a marriage companion, what may be more important than how he or she looks?

4. What is meant by this statement: "If a Christian marries a child of the devil he is going to have a lot of trouble with his father-in-law"?

5. What were the three restrictions of the Nazarite vow?

CHAPTER

6

The Thief That Has
Robbed Us All

Lesson text: Romans 3:23; 6:23
Memory verse: "All have sinned and come short of the glory of God" (Proverbs 3:23).

At some point in our lives, statistics tell us that most of us will be the victims of a thief (169.7 of every 1000 people in any given year). Perhaps your car, house, or wallet has already been violated by the hands of an uninvited visitor. Regardless, we can say with confidence that there is one thief who has made mockery of every mature person. His name is Sin.

Sin steals the innocence from one's mind. Adam and Eve were as innocent as babies and as pure as honey in the comb until the thief stole their innocence, as the wind steals the smoke (Genesis 3). Their unparalleled purity became as irreplaceable as a broken egg. They hid themselves from the God who had been their favorite companion. Their guilt drove them from their God, and their God drove them from their paradise. The age of innocence was finished.

Though under different circumstances and to varying degrees, the same thief has robbed us all of our innocence. Our purity lasts only until that thief, Sin, enters through the broken window of the mind or kicks in the door of the heart. When he leaves, he takes as loot the irretrievable treasure known as innocence. Until our lips have tasted the bitterness of alcohol, until our lungs have breathed nicotine's smoke, until our vessels have coursed with gambler's adrenaline, until our eyes have feasted on the indecent, until our fingers have handled dishonest gain, until our feet have known the sand of forbidden paths, until our bodies have slept in fornication's bed, until our tongues have known the curl of the curse word, until our hands have clenched into anger's fist, until our knees have bowed in prayer to the wrong god—*Until . . .* Once we give in, we can never say or think again, "I don't know what that sin is like."

Sin steals the comfort from one's pillow. Jacob pillowed his head on a stone, and found rest (Genesis 28:18), but the robbed man can seek rest on a goose-down feather pillow and find none (Proverbs 13:15; cf. Ecclesiastes 2:23; Romans 3:16–18). "There is no peace, saith the Lord, unto the wicked" (Isaiah 48:22). He lies on his bed wishing he could undo the past but knowing that the clock of life cannot be reversed. She closes her eyes to try to change the subject, but her mind flutters, lighting again on the same rotting carcass of sin's memory. He finally drifts into fitful sleep, only to waken with the first thought of the sin that is ever before him, wishing it were a dream but knowing it is all too real.

"The wicked man travaileth with pain all his days, and the number of years is hidden to the oppressor . . . Trouble and anguish shall make him afraid; they shall prevail against him, as a king ready to the battle" (Job 15:20–24). Rest comes hard to a conscience pricked with a thousand needles of guilt. What an evil and bitter thing sin is! (Jeremiah 2:19).

Sin steals the self-confidence from one's eye. The eye tells much about what a man thinks of himself. Jesus said, "The light of the body is the eye" (Matthew 6:22). As sins weigh on one's soul, it sometimes shows in his visual contact. Where once was a Christian confident in his power to wage war with Satan, now stands a sinner feeling like a prisoner of war. Where once stood a gymnast who had never fallen, now falters a girl who doubts her gracefulness. Where once stood the proud boxer whose knees had never buckled, now stands a man who hopes he can protect his chin. He is vulnerable, uncertain, and afraid the past may repeat itself.

Job had his confidence stolen during his suffering. He said, "If I justify myself, mine own mouth shall condemn me: if I say, I am perfect, it shall also prove me perverse" (Job 9:20). Jesus, though He looked not at them, found some who could not face Him because of the condemnation of their consciences: "And they which heard it, being convicted by their own conscience, went out one by one, beginning at the eldest, even unto the last: and Jesus was left alone, and the woman standing in the midst" (John 8:9; cf. Romans 2:1).

Sin steals the influence from one's life. The Christian worker who once owned the respect of his peers now feels like a hypocrite among associates (cf. Romans 2:21–24). The trusted friend who was once looked to for advice now finds that no one covets his counsel. The father whose sons once longed to walk in his steps finds that they have other heroes. The husband who once enjoyed the unreserved devotion of his wife now finds he is the recipient of suspicious questions and reluctant trust. The teen whose parents once trusted him completely now sees doubt in his father's eyes. Influence and trust, once lost, are difficult to rebuild.

Have you been visited by the thief? Get rid of your sins! God's wonderful grace has a plan for non-Christians to be free from sin: Faith, John 3:16; repentance, Luke 13:3; confession of Christ, Matthew 10:32; and baptism, Acts 2:38.

God's grace also has a plan for Christians who sin: Repentance, confession, prayer, Acts 8:22; James 5:16. Get rid of your guilt! Once God has forgotten your sins, you can forget them as well! "For if our heart condemn us, God is greater than our heart, and knoweth all things. Beloved, if our heart condemn us not, then have we confidence toward God" (1 John 3:20–21). Repentance will restore the innocence to your soul, the comfort to your pillow, the confidence to your eye, and the influence to your life.

Discussion Questions

1. What does this verse mean: "There is no peace, saith the Lord, unto the wicked"? (Isaiah 48:22).

2. Why is good influence one of a Christian's most valuable treasures? How quickly can a reputation be tarnished? How quickly can it be restored?

3. What does the phrase "give none occasion to the adversary to speak reproachfully" (1 Timothy 5:14) mean, and how does it apply to a young Christian's life?

4. Does sin usually stay "hidden"? Who usually finds out first?

5. How can a person get rid of sin's guilt?

Eli's Boys

Lesson text: 1 Samuel 2:12-22

Memory verse: "A wise son maketh a glad father: but a foolish son is the heaviness of his mother" (James 10:1).

Hophni and Phinehas learned about the downward spiral of sin. They grew up "in church." Their father was a priest; they became priests. They likely never missed a tabernacle service in their lives. Yet they turned out to be wicked. God even called them "vile" (1 Samuel 3:13).

What activities made them—and by extension youth today—vile in God's sight?

Eli's sons showed disrespect for worship (1 Samuel 2:12–16). The word *vile* here means "to make light of sacred things." Hophni and Phinehas made fun of God and made others dislike going to worship. What about my behavior in worship? Do I show disrespect for sacred things by remaining silent during singing, checking out everybody's clothes during the Lord's supper, passing the buck when passing the plate, getting a drink of water during the prayer, and passing notes or whispering during the sermon? If so, this disrespect displeases God.

Eli's sons threatened violence. They said, "I will take it by force" (1 Samuel 2:16). The words "violence" and "violent" are found sixty-five times in Scripture. You cannot find a lot of things that a loving God hates, but it can safely be said that the Lord hateth "him that loveth violence" (Psalm 11:5). There are some in every generation whom "violence covereth . . . as a garment" (Psalm 73:6) and who cannot sleep "except they have done mischief; and their sleep is taken away, unless they cause some to fall. For they eat the bread of wickedness, and drink the wine of violence" (Proverbs 4:16–17). In Noah's time, the earth was filled with violence (Genesis 6:11), which prompted God to destroy His own creation and drown His own children (6:13).

Moses' Law made provisions for those who were treated violently (Leviticus 6:2). Solomon warned his son to stay away from violent people, saying, "A violent man enticeth his neighbour, and leadeth him into the way that is not good" (Proverbs 16:29). God commanded, "Do no wrong, do no violence to the stranger, the fatherless, nor the widow, neither shed innocent blood in this place" (Jeremiah 22:3; cf. Ezekiel 45:9). God will "spare the poor and needy . . . [and] redeem their soul from deceit and violence" (Psalm 72:13–14; cf. Ecclesiastes 5:8).

John was concerned about violence. He commanded Roman soldiers: "Do violence to no man, neither accuse any falsely; and be content with your wages" (Luke 3:14). Jesus was a gentle man who would not quench smoking flax (Isaiah 42:3; Matthew 12:20) and did "no violence" (Isaiah 53:9). Even "the kingdom of heaven suffereth violence, and the violent take it by force" (Matthew 11:12), evidently referring to God's preachers (e.g., John, Jesus) being mistreated—ultimately murdered—by their enemies. Paul had to be rescued by soldiers because of "the violence of the people" (Acts 21:35).

In our society, humanistic thinking produces violent effects that in turn create an extremely violent nation. We murder babies in the womb and old people on their sickbeds. Gangs kill each other and innocent strangers in drive-by shootings. Road rage turns violent on our highways, and air rage turns violent at 35,000 feet. Drug growers set booby traps to ensnare law officers, and drug users rob citizens to get money for one more hit. Most schools have problems with fighting and guns in school. Don't turn to violence to solve your disagreements. Violence will just create new problems and will cause God's name to be discredited.

Eli's sons caused others to stumble. Because of them, "men abhorred the offering of the Lord" (1 Samuel 2:17). Paul admonished, "that no man put a stumblingblock or an occasion to fall in his brother's way . . . It is good neither to eat flesh, nor to drink wine, nor any thing whereby thy brother stumbleth, or is offended, or is made weak" (Romans 14:13–21). Jesus took the matter of stumbling seriously. He warned,

> Woe unto the world because of offences! for it must needs be that offences come; but woe to that man by whom the offence cometh! Wherefore if thy hand or thy foot offend thee, cut them off, and cast them from thee: it is better for thee to enter into life halt or maimed, rather than having two hands or two feet to be cast into everlasting fire. And if thine eye offend thee, pluck it out, and cast it from thee: it is better for thee to enter into life with one eye, rather than having two eyes to be cast into hell fire (Matthew 18:7–9).

We must be careful that our criticism of elders, preachers, Bible teachers, or the church does not discourage someone from attending (1 Corinthians 10:10). We must be careful that our clothing or behavior does not cause others to lust (1 Timothy 2:9; Matthew 5:28). We must be careful that our speech does not cause others to reject Christ (cf. Matthew 5:14–16; 26:74). God considers lying and hypocrisy vile behavior (Isaiah 32:6).

Jesus said, "It is impossible but that offences will come: but woe unto him, through whom they come! It were better for him that a millstone were hanged about his neck, and he cast into the sea, than that he should offend one of these little ones" (Luke 17:1–2). One reason God carried His people into captivity was that they had "caused them to stumble in their ways from the ancient paths" (Jeremiah 18:15; cf. 6:16).

Eli's sons committed sexual sin. "They lay with the women that assembled at the door of the tabernacle" (1 Samuel 2:22). In Jeremiah 15:19, a different word (*zalal*) is translated "vile," which means, "to shake (as in the wind), to be loose morally, worthless, or prodigal; glutton, riotous (eater)." This is the person we might call a "party animal" or that our parents might call a "fornicator." About half of teens admit to committing fornication by high school graduation. You will be tempted to commit this sin before you get married—perhaps many times.

Please remember that fornication is a sin with serious consequences—in immediate, lifelong, and eternal terms. It scars the mind with guilt, hardens the heart with embarrassment, damages the body with disease, limits the future with pregnancy, and affects future spouses with jealousy and sexual dysfunction. It is little wonder that Paul wrote, "Flee fornication. Every sin that a man doeth is without the body; but he that committeth fornication sinneth against his own body" (1 Corinthians 6:18). He added, "Flee also youthful lusts" (2 Timothy 2:22).

Sexual temptation does not cease with marriage. Adultery is not something to be toyed with. Although about fifteen percent of married Americans have affairs, "let it not be once named among" God's people (Ephesians 5:3). It brings serious shame to the church for a member to be overcome in such a fault (Hebrews 6:6). It causes untold heartache to innocent spouses; it is treacherous (Malachi 2:14; Matthew 19:9). The divorce it often leads to leaves children with serious emotional scars. It leaves society weakened economically and morally (Proverbs 14:34). It is little wonder that the wise man said, "But whoso committeth adultery with a woman lacketh understanding: he that doeth it destroyeth his own soul. A wound and dishonour shall he get; and his reproach shall not be wiped away" (Proverbs 6:32–33).

If Hophni and Phinehas' heterosexual sin ("they lay with the women") was "vile," then what does God think of lesbianism and homosexuality? We are not left to wonder, for He also refers to these actions as "vile" (Judges 19:24). Paul wrote, "For this cause God gave them up unto vile affections: for even their women did change the natural use into that which is against nature" (Romans 1:26). The word *vile* here means, "disgrace; dishonor, reproach, shame." Through politics, academia, media, and false religion, political correctness presently pushes Christians to accept homosexuality. However, since God has not changed His opinion, we must not change ours!

Hophni and Phineas show that growing up "in church" does not necessarily mean one will end up in heaven (1 Samuel 3:13).

Discussion Questions

1. How seriously does God take showing disrespect for worship? How can I show my respect for God during worship services?

2. Give some examples of how humanistic thinking in our society produces violence. How can we protect ourselves? How can we avoid turning to violence to settle disputes?

3. What does it mean to "put a stumbling block or an occasion to fall in his brother's way"? (Romans 14:13). Give some examples.

4. What does God think of lesbianism and homosexuality? (Read Romans 1:24–28)

5. Explain what this means: "First we toy with sin, and then sin toys with us."

6. Read and explain James 1:12–15.

Simon Says

Lesson text: Luke 7:36-50

Memory verse: "Abstain from all appearance of evil" (1 Thessalonians 5:22).

Jesus had an unusual lunch one day with a Pharisee named Simon (Luke 7:36-50). During the course of the meal, a prostitute (*harmartolos*, "sinner, a notoriously bad woman") came into the courtyard and approached Jesus. What then occurred is one of the most interesting encounters in Jesus' visit to earth.

Since the custom was to remove sandals and recline on pillows while eating, when she came up behind Jesus, she stood over His bare feet. Evidently overwhelmed with joy at the thought of turning her life around, she began to weep, and her tears fell on His feet. She noticed that they had not been washed by the host (a common custom), so she bent down and began to wipe them clean with the hairs of her head. (Picture this!). While she bathed His feet with her tears, she began to kiss them, expressing gratitude for what He had done (the Greek verb tense in 7:48 indicates she had already been forgiven).

All this, as you might imagine, was quite embarrassing to Simon! Under normal circumstances, he would not even walk on the same street with this woman. Now she's on his property, affectionately greeting his Guest . . . what should he do? How can he graciously handle this situation? Why was Jesus letting her do this?

Simon used the circumstances to form an opinion about the validity of Jesus' claim to be a prophet. He figured no true prophet would allow such a woman to touch him, so He either did not know what kind of woman she was (thus lacking a prophet's discernment) or knew and did not care (thus lacking a prophet's holiness). Simon's conclusion: Jesus was no prophet.

Of course, Simon did not verbalize these thoughts to his Guest, but the whole time he was thinking them, Jesus was reading his mind. He said more than he meant to say that day. In fact, Simon is still "saying" today.

Simon says, "Pretend you're not a sinner."

It is too bad that this woman fell into sin, but it is even worse that Simon was living in sin and did not know it. In the Sermon on the Mount (Matthew 5-7) and in Matthew 23, Jesus rebuked the Pharisees for self-righteousness and an unwillingness to admit sin. The Pharisee in one of Jesus' parables (typical of many Pharisees) felt that God was his debtor rather than the other way around (Luke 18:10-11).

It is interesting to note that those who walked closest to God saw their sinfulness the clearest. Abraham considered himself "but dust and ashes" (Genesis 18:27). God confessed Job to be "perfect and upright" (Job 1:1); yet Job confessed to God, "Behold, I am vile" (40:4). Ezra prayed, "O my God, I am ashamed and blush to lift up my face" (9:6). Peter fell to his knees and begged the Lord, "Depart from me, for I am a sinful man" (Luke 5:8), and when John saw the glorified Christ, he fell at His feet as a dead man (Revelation 1:17). Paul called himself the chief of sinners (1 Timothy 1:15).

The whole point of the parable Jesus told Simon about the two debtors is that all men are sinners whether they feel guilty or not. Both of the men were in debt and bankrupt. The difference between five-hundred pence and fifty pence is not a difference in guilt. The two amounts represent a difference in their sense of guilt. The woman was not more lost than the Pharisee. How much sin does a person have to commit in order to be a sinner? Ten sins or a hundred? "For whosoever shall keep the whole law, and yet offend in one point, he is guilty of all" (James 2:10). The prostitute was better than the Pharisee because she would admit and turn from her sin. Simon says, "Pretend you don't have any sins and they will go away" (but Simon is wrong).

Simon says, "Pretend a sin's not a sin unless you do it."

Simon knew what the woman had done but forgot what he had not done. She was guilty of committing sin; he was guilty of omitting righteousness. He had not even shown Jesus common courtesy—the kiss of welcome, water for His feet, and oil for His head (cf. Genesis 18:1-8.) God may condemn us for what we did not do. "Therefore to him that knoweth to do good, and doeth it not, to him it is sin" (James 4:17). Omission can be as sinful as commission. One who does not do what God requires is as guilty as the one who does what God forbids. Simon says, "Ignoring God's commands is better than breaking them" (but Simon is wrong).

Simon says, "Act like the other fellow's sins are worse than yours."

Evidently, the woman had been guilty of blatant sexual sins (cf. 2 Corinthians 7:1; Galatians 5:19-21). She was a sinner. Simon knew it; she knew it; Jesus knew it; everybody knew it. Simon, too, was a sinner, only he didn't know it. He was not guilty of immorality but of sins of attitude (unfair judging, for instance, Matthew 7:1-2).

The Pharisees practiced "respectable sins" like hypocrisy and pride (Matthew 23:23; 12:24-34). They condemned others to exalt themselves. They coveted not only money (Luke 16:14) but also prestige and praise. They practiced their religion only to be seen of men (Matthew 6:5: 23:5). Such sins won't keep you out of polite company, but they will keep you out of heaven. These sins most likely won't cause the church to withdraw fellowship from one, but they will cause God to withhold His favor. Simon says, "Sins of the flesh are worse than sins of the spirit" (but Simon is wrong).

Simon says, "Don't worry about the sins that nobody knows about."

To Simon, open sins were worse than hidden sins. If nobody knows about it, then don't sweat it. Everyone at the feast knew who the woman was and what she had done. Her sins were open. But only Jesus (who can read hearts, John 2:25) knew Simon's sins. Simon was conscious of no need, felt no love, and so received no forgiveness. His impression of himself was that he was a good man in the sight of God and men. The woman was conscious of nothing else than an immediate need for forgiveness. The Pharisee, who sought no forgiveness, obtained what he sought.

To be forgiven of sin and to become a Christian, God asks us to believe in His Son Jesus (Acts 16:31), repent of sins (Luke 13:3), confess faith in Christ (Romans 10:10), and be baptized for the remission of sins (Acts 2:38). He then asks us to worship and serve Him faithfully (John 4:24; Hebrews 10:25; Revelation 2:10). Simon says, "If it's hidden, it's covered" (but Simon is wrong).

Don't play with Simon; he'll get you in trouble.

Discussion Questions

1. What did the woman in this story do to Jesus that was unusual?

2. Does it do any good (ultimately) for sinners to pretend they do not have sins?

3. What is the point of Jesus parable about two debtors?

4. Name some sins a person may commit without "doing" anything.

5. Should we be concerned about the sins no one knows about?

CHAPTER

9

What the Bible Says About Salvation

Lesson text: Acts 2

Memory verse: "He that believeth and is baptized shall be saved; but he that believeth not shall be damned" (Mark 16:16).

Salvation is the theme of the Bible. The first prophecy of Christ was spoken soon after Adam and Eve sinned (Genesis 3:15). Jesus said that He came to seek and save the lost (Luke 19:10).

The Bible says that all mature people are sinners (Romans 3:23) and that all sinners are lost without Christ (Romans 6:23; Isaiah 59:1–2). Since each of us will one day stand before the judgment seat of Christ (2 Corinthians 5:10), we need a Savior.

The Bible presents salvation as having two sides: God's part, and man's part. God, because of His great love for mankind, has done His part in sending Christ to die for the sins of men. The Bible says, "God commendeth his love toward us, in that, while we were yet sinners, Christ died for us" (Romans 5:8). God's part is called grace: "For by grace are ye saved through faith; and that not of yourselves: it is the gift of God" (Ephesians 2:8). Paul explains that we cannot save ourselves, and that we must rely on God's grace.

No person is ready to be judged on his own goodness or morality (cf. Isaiah 64:6).

"Through faith" means that man must also do his part, because no one benefits from a gift until he receives it. Man's part in salvation initially involves obedience to God's five simple requirements for salvation.

First, sinners must learn about Jesus Christ. The Savior said, "No man can come to me, except the Father which hath sent me draw him: and I will raise him up at the last day. It is written in the prophets, And they shall be all taught of God. Every man therefore that hath heard, and hath learned of the Father, cometh unto me" (John 6:44–45).

We need to hear and understand enough of the details of Jesus' life (birth, teachings, miracles, character, death, resurrection) to be fully convinced that He is God's Son. Paul said, "So then faith cometh by hearing, and hearing by the word of God" (Romans 10:17). We may hear by listening to lessons from the Bible or by studying the Bible, especially Matthew, Mark, Luke, and John.

Second, sinners must believe in Jesus Christ as God's Son. The Savior said, "For God so loved the world, that he gave his only begotten Son, that whosoever believeth in him should not perish, but have everlasting life" (John 3:16). Also, "I said therefore unto you, that ye shall die in your sins: for if ye believe not that I am he, ye shall die in your sins" (John 8:24). We must believe that Jesus

- existed on earth and preexisted in heaven (John 1:1–3, 14).

- was a great teacher (John 3:2; 7:46) who commands belief in His teachings (Matthew 28:20).

- was a good man and that He was sinless (John 8:46; Hebrews 4:15).

- was a prophet of God, yea, more than a prophet (cf. Luke 7:26).

- was a miracle-worker (Matthew 8; 15:30), and One on whom miracles were worked—for instance, the virgin birth and indwelling of the Spirit (Matthew 1:18–25; 3:16).

- was killed by the Jews and Romans, buried in Joseph's borrowed tomb, and resurrected early Sunday morning (Matthew 26–28).

- has returned to His Father and will one day come back to take us home with Him (John 14:1–6; Acts 1:9–11).

Few people would deny that a good man named Jesus lived on the earth and taught important principles that are helpful. Others would concede that Jesus might have been a prophet. These people "believe" in the sense of "acknowledgement of facts," but they do not have the kind of faith God expects Christians to have.

In the eighteenth century, the U.S. Congress issued a special edition of Thomas Jefferson's Bible. Jefferson had excised all references to the supernatural so that it simply contained Jesus' moral teachings. The closing words of Jesus' life in this Bible were, "There laid they Jesus and rolled a great stone at the mouth of the sepulcher and departed." We end up with a dead philosopher rather than a risen Lord when we limit the Scriptures to what is easy for us to believe.

To doubt Jesus' miracles and resurrection is to deny God's power. If God was not strong enough to raise His own Son, what hope is there for an afterlife for the rest of us? (cf. 1 Corinthians 15). A God that can make a universe, create life, flood the earth, part a sea, and stop the sun can surely raise His beloved, sinless Son from a grave.

In short, we must believe (have faith) that Jesus of Nazareth is nothing less than the Son of God! On Pentecost, the Jews heard the gospel and "were pricked in their heart, and said unto Peter and to the rest of the apostles, Men and brethren, what shall we do?" (Acts 2:37). Their question, "What shall we do?" showed that they believed the message, but they realized that they needed to do more than have simple belief to reach salvation. James wrote, "Ye see then how that by works a man is justified, and not by faith only" (James 2:24).

Third, a sinner must repent of sins. The Savior said, "Except ye repent, ye shall all likewise perish" (Luke 13:3). His ambassador added,

"Repent, and be baptized every one of you in the name of Jesus Christ for the remission of sins" (Acts 2:38). Repentance means "a change of mind that produces a change in behavior" (cf. 2 Corinthians 7:10). In simple terms, it means to give up on sinful living and to start living to please Christ. It means to stop serving Satan and self, and start serving God and others (cf. Philippians 2:1–8).

Fourth, a sinner must confess faith in Christ (Romans 10:9–10). We must verbalize what we have come to believe in our hearts. We should make the same confession the Ethiopian treasurer made before he climbed down from his chariot to be baptized: "I believe that Jesus Christ is the Son of God" (Acts 8:37). A confession of belief in Christ on earth will trigger a similar (think of it!) event in heaven—Jesus will confess us before His Father and the angels. The Savior said, "Whosoever therefore shall confess me before men, him will I confess also before my Father which is in heaven" (Matthew 10:32). Amazing! You and I may never know or be known by anyone famous on earth, but every angel in heaven will know our names. The president of our country may not know us, but the One who presides in heaven will.

Fifth, a sinner must be baptized in water for the forgiveness of sins. The Savior said, "He that believeth and is baptized shall be saved; but he that believeth not shall be damned" (Mark 16:16). Baptism is the final step in leaving the world (Satan's domain) and becoming a part of the church (Christ's kingdom) (Galatians 3:26–27). God chose to remove our past sins (Acts 22:16; 1 Peter 3:21) through baptism and give us His Son's name to wear (cf. Acts 11:26).

Is it really necessary to be baptized in water in order to go to heaven? Many religious people scoff at the idea. Let's allow God's Word to answer this question. The book of Acts explains God's plan of salvation through several examples of conversion. It records nine specific accounts of conversion:

- The Jews on Pentecost, Chapter 2
- The Samaritans, Chapter 8
- The Ethiopian eunuch, Chapter 8
- Saul of Tarsus, Chapters 9 and 22

- Cornelius, Chapter 10
- Lydia, Chapter 16
- The Philippian jailer, Chapter 16
- The Corinthians, Chapter 18
- The Ephesians, Chapter 19.

In each example, the people who became Christians took certain common actions or steps of obedience. Each was taught about Jesus before conversion; each became a believer in Him; each repented; each confessed; each was baptized into Christ. Following conversion to Christ, each Christian was required to grow strong in Christ and remain faithful to Him (cf. Acts 8:22; Revelation 2:10).

Twenty-seven times in Acts—the book of conversions—one finds the words *baptized* and *baptism*. Anytime someone asked what he needed to do in order to be saved, baptism was always a part of the answer. For example, on the first day of the church's existence (the Day of Pentecost), the people with tender consciences who heard Peter's preaching were told to "repent, and be baptized . . . for the remission of sins" (Acts 2:38). Note that baptism was for the remission of sins. To say that baptism is unessential is to argue that having one's sins remitted (forgiven) is unessential.

Later in Acts, we find the word "must" connected with baptism on two occasions. On the road to Damascus, Saul was told to go into the city where it would be told him what he "must do" to please Jesus (Acts 9:6). In the city he was told to arise and "wash away" his sins by being baptized (Acts 22:16; cf. 1 Corinthians 6:11).

Later, the Philippian jailor asked what he "must do" to be saved (Acts 16:30). He was instructed to believe on Jesus to be saved (16:31). When Paul and Silas taught him about belief, they must have talked about baptism, because he was baptized the same hour of the night (16:33). Note that he rejoiced after baptism, an indication of his joy of having sins forgiven (16:34).

It is interesting that baptism is the only step toward salvation explicitly mentioned in every conversion account (Acts 2:38; 8:12; 8:13; 9:18; 22:16; 10:48; 16:15; 16:33; 18:8; 19:5). Since God is no respecter of persons (Acts

10:34–35; Romans 2:11), what He requires of one person to be saved, He requires of all. What He required then, He requires now.

We urge you to study carefully these Scriptures in your own Bible. See whether these things are so (Acts 17:11); be "fully persuaded in [your] own mind" (Romans 14:5); and "work out your own salvation with fear and trembling" (Philippians 2:12). If you have questions that you would like to study further, talk with your bible teacher, preacher, or parents. If you are not attending the church of Christ, the local preacher or youth minister will be happy to talk with you (look it up in the phone book or on the Web).

Discussion Questions

1. Reread the story of the prodigal son in Luke 15. How do we know the young man's father was watching for his return? How does God watch for sinners to return?

2. Compare and contrast the attitudes of Eve, Jonah, David, and Samson with the attitudes of Joseph, Moses, Ruth, and Samuel. What can we learn from the choices each one of them made?

3. Discuss the steps listed to become a Christian. How do these instructions from the Bible differ from instructions you have heard from denominations about what one must do to be saved?

Trust and Obey,
For There is No Other Way

Lesson text: 1 Samuel 3:10

Memory verse: "Submit yourselves therefore to God. Resist the devil, and he will flee from you" (James 4:7).

Baptism is not the end of obedience to God; it is the beginning. Romans 6:4 explains that "we are buried with him by baptism into death: that like as Christ was raised up from the dead by the glory of the Father, even so we also should walk in newness of life." The old person who lived a lifestyle of sin died in the grave of baptism; a new, clean, forgiven Christian is resurrected. Of course, Christians still sin, but sin will no longer be our habit or lifestyle. We will work each day to become more and more like Jesus, a process the Bible calls "walking in the light" (1 John 1:7).

Another image of the life God calls us to live is found in the Old Testament. In Jeremiah 18, God tells the prophet to watch a potter shaping a vessel out of clay. The vessel was marred or defective, but the potter reshaped it into a useful vessel. Then God said, "Behold, as the clay is in the potter's hand, so are ye in mine hand, O house of Israel" (Jeremiah 18:6). Israel was caught up in sin, but God through Jeremiah told them to repent. Once we repent and submit to God in baptism and in the way we live our lives, He can shape us into the kind of people He wants us to be—holy, pure, perfect (complete) images of Christ (1 Peter 2:5, 9; Romans 12:1–2).

Adelaide A. Pollard wrote the beautiful hymn, "Have Thine Own Way Lord" in 1908. Born in Iowa in 1862, Miss Pollard, an accomplished poet and prose writer, was convinced that God wanted her to go to Africa as a missionary. She was dejected when she was unable to raise enough funds.

About this time, she attended a women's prayer meeting and heard an elderly woman pray: "But it's all right, Lord. It does not matter what you bring into our lives, just have your way with us!" Later that evening while meditating on the story of the potter in Jeremiah 18, Pollard recalled that humble prayer. It inspired her, and within minutes she wrote all four stanzas of the hymn. A year later, the noted composer George C. Stebbins put the poem to the tune and harmony we sing still today. A Christian's philosophy can be summed up in the words of Miss Pollard's hymn:

> Have Thine own way, Lord! Have Thine own way!
> Thou art the Potter; I am the clay.
> Mold me and make me after Thy will,
> While I am waiting, yielded and still.
> Have Thine own way, Lord! Have Thine own way!
> Search me and try me, Master, today!
> Whiter than snow, Lord, wash me just now,
> As in Thy presence, humbly I bow.
> Have Thine own way, Lord! Have Thine own way!
> Hold o'er my being absolute sway!
> Fill with Thy spirit till all shall see
> Christ only, always, living in me!

As Christians, how do we meet this daily challenge of allowing God to "mold and make" us into the image of Christ? The answer may be in the simple chorus of another familiar hymn:

Trust and obey, for there's no other way
To be happy in Jesus, but to trust and obey.

We Can Trust God

It's difficult to trust when we can't see what's ahead, isn't it? A pilot was having difficulty landing his small airplane since fog hid the runway, so the airport decided to bring it in by radar. As he received instructions, he suddenly recalled a tall pole in his flight path. Panic-stricken he feverishly appealed to the control tower. A blunt reply came back, "You obey instructions, we'll take care of obstructions." In a similar way, the Bible urges, "Trust in the Lord with all thine heart; and lean not unto thine own understanding. In all thy ways acknowledge him, and he shall direct thy paths" (Proverbs 3:5–6).

The young Samuel answered, "Here am I," the most natural response to God (Genesis 22:1; Exodus 3:4). This is the answer that all should make. It expresses trust—the surrender of our will to God's. It was a strange, long road on which Samuel put his foot that day. He did not know where it was to lead him—and neither do we when we become Christians. We may end up missionaries in a far land. We may become preachers (or married to preachers). We may serve in hospitals or Christian schools.

We do not need to know at the beginning where God's work will take us. It is enough to trust God with tomorrow. We get the details bit by bit as we learn the Word more perfectly and see the doors of opportunity that God opens. The surrender must be entire at the beginning, though. It is false obedience which says, "Tell me first everything that I will be asked to do, and then I will see whether or not I will do it." The true spirit of submission says, "'I delight to do thy will' (Psalm 40:8); now show me what it is." Let us accept God's laws in bulk now, and later accept each single one as we learn it.

A television program preceding the Winter Olympics one year featured blind skiers being trained for slalom skiing, as impossible as it sounds. Paired with sighted skiers, the blind skiers were taught on the flats how to make right and left turns. When that was mastered, they were taken to the slalom slope, where their sighted partners skied beside them, shouting, "Left!" and, "Right!"

As they obeyed the commands, they were able to negotiate the course and cross the finish line, depending solely on the sighted skier's word. It was either complete trust or catastrophe. What a vivid picture of the Christian life!

We Can Trust the Bible

It starts out subtilely. The religious characters in the TV shows are always a little weird. News reports focus on aberrations in the "Christian community"—people who either live in the past, or are strange, simple, offbeat people, or are hypocrites who don't practice what they preach. In college it becomes more blatant. A biology professor or a psychology teacher comes right out and makes fun of anyone who still believes the Bible is anything more than a mistake-filled collection of ancient Jewish sayings.

You won't get through your freshman year without being told that belief in God is for the back-woodsy, uneducated—though perhaps well-meaning—folks back home. It belongs to those who still use typewriters, think CDs are something you put in a bank, and that IPODs must be some kind of plant, or something NASA invented. It is not for a person who is educated and intelligent. Only the uninformed, ignorant, or unbalanced believe the Bible. No one takes anyone seriously who takes the Bible seriously.

So what about that?

Let's start at the beginning: Do you believe in God? "My parents do, I think. My grandmother does for sure. Everybody at church does, so I guess I do. I mean, everybody believes in God, don't they?"

No, you will find some who positively don't. And unless you absolutely do, then you may end up on their side.

Each person has to examine the evidence and decide for himself what he believes. She can't get by on her parent's faith or go to heaven on her preacher's coattails. You've got to make up your mind if you really believe in God and His Son Jesus or if you believe in evolution and its "son" Humanism.

Don't be intimidated by unbelieving philosophers, professors, or scientists. An intelligent, educated person can—and should—believe in God and in the Bible as His Word. Some of the world's greatest men—whose intelligence is indisputable—were believers.

The short list of big achievers

Many of the major branches of science were founded by Bible believers. It is intriguing that the five greatest physicists in history (Newton, Faraday, Thompson, Maxwell, Einstein) were outspoken in their conviction that the universe was placed here by a Creator.

A short list of famous scientists who believed in creation include: Robert Boyle—scientist and chemist; Michael Faraday—physicist, formulated laws of electromagnetic induction, did groundwork for making dynamos, electric motors, and transformers; James Joule—science of thermodynamics; William Thompson (a.k.a. Lord Kelvin)—thermodynamics and the Kelvin temperature scale; Johannes Kepler—laws of planetary motion; Carl Linnaeus—botanist, professor; Matthew Maury—leading scientist in oceanography and hydrography; James Clerk Maxwell—electromagnetic theory; Samuel F. B. Morse—invented the telegraph (Morse code is named after him); Isaac Newton—laws of gravity, motion and calculus; Blaise Pascal—invented early calculator, helped discover the theory of probability; Louis Pasteur—invented vaccination, immunization, and pasteurization; Sir Henry Rawlinson—archaeologist; George Stokes—physicist and mathematician.

Pretty impressive, company, wouldn't you say?

Did you hear the one about the three astronauts at Christmas?

On Christmas Day 1968, the three astronauts of Apollo 8 circled the dark side of the moon and headed home. Suddenly, over the horizon of the moon rose the blue and white earth, garlanded by the glistening light of the sun against the black void of space. Those sophisticated men, trained in science and technology, did not utter Einstein's name. No one heard them say "Sagan" or "Hawking." They did not go to the poets, the lyricists, or the dramatists. Only one thing could capture the awe-inspiring thrill of this magnificent observation. Billions heard the voice from outer space as the astronaut read: "In the beginning God created the heaven and the earth"—the only concept worthy enough to describe that unspeakable awe.[1]

What about the Harvard astronomer?

Harvard astronomer Owen Gingerish commented on NASA's Cosmic Background Explorer (COBE) satellite which provided scientists with a wealth of information. Scientists reported on the satellite's $400 million mission to study the universe's origins. After more than 300 million measurements by COBE, the research scientists noted how closely their new discovery of the universe's creation compared with the biblical account. Gingerish said,

> Both the contemporary scientific account and the age-old biblical account assume a beginning, and its essential framework, of everything springing forth from that blinding flash, bears a striking resonance with those succinct words of Genesis 1:3: "And God said, Let there be light."[2]

Frederic Burnham, science historian and Director of The Trinity Institute in New York City, said many scientists would, at this time more than any time in the last one hundred years, consider the idea that God created the universe a respectable hypothesis.[3]

Have you ever heard of any of these?

- SIR ISAAC NEWTON: This most beautiful system of the sun, planets, and comets, could only proceed from the counsel and dominion of an intelligent and powerful Being. This Being governs all things, not as the soul of the world, but as Lord over all; and on account of his dominion he is wont to be called Lord God . . . I find more sure marks of authenticity in the Bible than in any profane history whatever.[4]

- RALPH WALDO EMERSON: Jesus is the most perfect of all men that have yet appeared.[5]

- CHARLES DICKENS (in his will): I commit my soul to the mercy of God, through our Lord and Saviour Jesus Christ, and exhort my dear children humbly to try to guide themselves by the teachings of the New Testament.[6]

- SHAKESPEARE (in his will): I commend my soul into the hands of God, my Creator, hoping and assuredly believing, through the only merits of Jesus my Saviour, to be made partaker of life everlasting.[7]

- GEORGE WASHINGTON: It is impossible [for a man] to rightly govern the world without God and the Bible . . . He is worse than an infidel who does not read his Bible and acknowledge his obligation to God.[8]

- JOHN ADAMS: The Bible is the best Book in the world.[9]

- BENJAMIN FRANKLIN: Young man, my advice to you is that you cultivate an acquaintance with and firm belief in the Holy Scriptures, for this is your certain interest. I think Christ's system of morals and religion, as He left them with us, is the best the world ever saw or is likely to see.[10]

- THOMAS JEFFERSON: I have always said and always will say that the studious perusal of the Sacred Volume will make better citizens, better fathers, better husbands . . . The Bible makes the best people in the world.[11]

- JOHN QUINCY ADAMS: My custom is to read four or five chapters of the Bible every morning immediately after rising . . . It seems to me the most suitable manner of beginning the day . . . It is an invaluable and inexhaustible mine of knowledge and virtue.[12]

- ABRAHAM LINCOLN: I am profitably engaged in reading the Bible. Take all of this Book upon reason that you can, and the balance by faith, and you will live and die a better man.[13]

- WOODROW WILSON: I have a very simple thing to ask of you. I ask every man and woman in this audience that from this day on they will realize that part of the destiny of America lies in their daily perusal of this great Book.[14]

- WILLIAM PENN: The Scriptures contain a declaration of the mind and will of God. . . . They ought also to be read, believed, and fulfilled in our day. We accept them as the words of God himself.[15]

- DANIEL WEBSTER: From the time that, at my mother's feet or on my father's knee, I first learned to lisp the verses from the sacred writings, they have been my daily study and vigilant contemplation.[16]

- DOUGLAS MACARTHUR: Believe me, sir, never a night goes by, be I ever so tired, but I read the Word of God before I go to bed.[17]

- WILLIAM E. GLADSTONE: I have known ninety-five great men of the world in my time, and of these, eighty-seven were all followers of the Bible.[18]

So what do you believe in if you don't believe in God? Yourself—and evolution. To believe that man evolved from lower life forms requires belief in spontaneous generation—that life came from non-life—which was long ago disproved by science. From nothing comes . . . nothing. We have something; therefore, something has always existed. There are but two possibilities: mind or matter. Which is more plausible: that dead, lifeless, inanimate matter brought this complicated world into existence, or that there was an eternal, intelligent, powerful mind behind the creation of the universe? Surely the latter. As Isaac Bashevis Singer said, "A number of materialistic thinkers have ascribed to blind evolution more miracles, more improbable coincidences and wonders, than all the teleologists could ever devise."

For one to say, "There is no God," he must be omnipotent, omniscient, and omnipresent—all-powerful, all-knowing, and everywhere at the same time. Otherwise, the power he does not have may be the power of God; the place where he is not may be the place where God is; and the knowledge that he does not have may be the knowledge of God.

Some doubt God's existence since He is not perceptible to our sensory system. According to this reasoning, we would have to repudiate one's conscience, molecular adhesion, and gravity. Just because I have never seen Katmandu doesn't mean it is not at the base of Everest.

Howard Hendricks observed, "There is no such thing as a correspondence course for swimming." If you want to swim you must get into the pool. It is the same in the world of ideas. You cannot remain neutral on the question of the existence of God and the Bible as His Word. Test the water.

Truly, "The fool hath said in his heart, There is no God" (Psalm 14:1).

Parade Magazine once carried a story about a little village church in Kalinovka, Russia, where attendance at Sunday school picked up after the minister started handing out candy to the peasant children. One of the most faithful was a pug-nosed, pugnacious lad who recited his Scriptures with proper devotion, pocketed his reward, and then fled to the fields to munch on it.

The minister took a liking to the boy and persuaded him to attend church school. He preferred doing this to household chores, so he went. By offering other rewards, the teacher managed to teach the boy all the verses of Matthew, Mark, Luke, and John. He won a special prize for learning all four by heart and reciting them nonstop in a church service. Sixty years later, he still liked to recite Scriptures, but in a context that would horrify his old teacher. You see, the prize pupil who memorized so much of the Bible was Nikita Khrushchev, the late communist ruler!

Had Khrushchev come to understand and appreciate the great truths he worked so diligently to memorize, how different the attitude of the whole country of Russia might have been. But all his efforts were only "building on the sand." Jesus said (in some of the verses Khrushchev memorized), "And every one that heareth these sayings of mine, and doeth them not, shall be likened unto a foolish man, which built his house upon the sand: and the rain descended, and the floods came, and the winds blew, and beat upon the house; and it fell: and great was the fall of it" (Matthew 7:26–27).

We all recognize the tragedy of one's failure to become a Christian when he has learned the truth. But the person who boasts of how much he has read the Bible and then has to be begged to be faithful to the Lord may be worse off in the judgment than one who knew little or nothing about the truth.

Discussion Questions

1. How is the Christian's life like clay in the potter's hands? How do we sometimes prevent God from shaping us?

2. What lessons can we learn from the hymn "Have Thine Own Way, Lord"?

3. What lessons can we learn from the hymn "Trust and Obey"?

4. What other songs teach us to depend on God?

5. When Satan tempts us, he promises pleasure and success. What did the prodigal son learn about the results of sin?

6. The Bible says that the prodigal son "came to himself." What does that mean? Can you give an example of someone who "came to himself" and changed his behavior?

7. What does it mean to trust God?

8. Can the Bible be trusted as a guide to heaven?

9. Can the Bible be trusted as a guide to behavior in this life?

10. Can an intelligent person believe the Bible? Name some brilliant scientists and philosophers who had faith in Scripture.

A Better Way

Lesson text: Mark 10:21; Hebrews 5:8-9
Memory verse: "Be doers of the word, and not hearers only, deceiving your own selves" (James 1:22).

A father was concerned that his son, who always seemed to be in hot water, would get into serious trouble when he got older. He worked on ways to change his behavior. Finally he came up with the idea that struck a cord with the boy. Every time the boy got into trouble, he was sent out with a hammer to drive a nail into a post his father had placed in the front yard. It was not many days until the post looked like a porcupine. After a week, the boy began to act better and seemed concerned about the nails in the post.

Finally he approached his father and asked how they could be removed. He thought for a moment and said, "Every time you do a good deed, I'll let you take one out." He seemed pleased and in a few days all the nails were gone. Still, his father saw him staring at the post. He asked him why, once there were no nails in the post.

The boy said, "The nail scars are still there."

So it is. We can remove sin's guilt, but its scars may remain for a long time.

A much better way is to learn to obey God while young, and never experience the pain of sin. But just what does it mean to "obey God"? James wrote, "Be doers of the word, and not hearers only, deceiving your own selves" (James 1:22).

What is Obedience?

Obedience is doing what God has said. Jacob told Esau, "Now therefore, my son, obey my voice according to that which I command thee" (Genesis 27:8). James wrote, "Whoso looketh into the perfect law of liberty, and continueth therein, he being not a forgetful hearer, but a doer of the work, this man shall be blessed in his deed" (James 1:25). Obedience is not:
- doing what others say,
- doing what others say God has said,
- doing what one wishes God had said,
- or doing what one thinks God has said.

It is simply doing what God says.

Obedience is doing only what God has said (Deuteronomy 4:2; cf. 12:32; 1 Corinthians 4:6; Revelation 22:18). Have you ever heard a young person say, "Well, the Bible doesn't say not to do it"? Those who want to gamble, drink a little, smoke marijuana, and go parking with boyfriends or girlfriends have been known to use this argument.

There is a borderline between sin and righteousness. We should not try to get as close as possible to it without going over. A wise teen or adult stays a healthy distance from sin. After Paul listed the sins of the flesh, he said "and such like" (Galatians 5:21), showing that anything borderline to one of these sins should be avoided.

The word *church* means "the called out from the kingdom of sin." John said, "Love not the world, neither the things that are in the world. If any man love the world, the love of the Father is not in him" (1 John 2:15). One who seeks to stay just as near the world of sin as possible and still follow

Christ has the wrong attitude. Paul wrote, "Abhor that which is evil; cleave to that which is good" (Romans 12:9).

Obedience is doing only what God has said in the way God has said (Matthew 7:21; John 12:48; 15:14; 1 John 3:22; Revelation 22:14). Take the command to be baptized (Mark 16:16), for instance. Some say they are "baptized," but they only have a little water sprinkled or poured on them (cf. Romans 6:3–4). They have not obeyed God in the way He said to be baptized. Others are immersed, but they say the purpose is "to show that they have already been saved" instead of "for the remission of sins" (Acts 2:38; 22:16). They have not obeyed God in the way He said do it.

Another example is the Lord's supper. Some take the Lord's supper, but they only have unleavened bread and no juice (Matthew 26:26–29). Or they partake of it only once in a while and not every week (cf. Acts 20:7). Or they take it on a day other than Sunday (Acts 20:7; cf. 1 Corinthians 11; 16:1–2). These practices are not obeying God in the way He said do it.

Obedience does not mean sinless perfection (1 John 1:8–10), but it does mean we must obey from a pure heart for the right reasons, or our obedience is vain. Amaziah "did that which was right in the sight of the Lord, but not with a perfect heart" (2 Chronicles 25:2). If we obey God to be seen of men and praised by them (Matthew 6), or just because of what's in it for us (Matthew 20:1–16; Hosea 1:4), we obey for the wrong reasons, and God will not be pleased. The right reasons for obedience are to glorify God (Matthew 5:16), to receive His praise (Matthew 6:4), and to express our trust and thanksgiving (Matthew 20:1–16).

Obedience is doing all that God said. The American Standard Version translates Psalm 119:160 as, "The sum of thy word is truth; and every one of thy righteous ordinances endureth forever." The New King James Version says, "The entirety of Your word is truth." Jesus' mother once gave some good advice that we should still follow today: "Whatsoever he saith unto you, do it" (John 2:5).

One of the most dangerous words in the English language is *partial.* After a snowstorm, the news may report that the streets have been partially cleared. Those few patches of snow and ice are still treacherous. In fact, the cleared spots can cause us to be too confident about our ability to navigate. To partially obey God is to disobey him. In 1 Samuel 15, Saul tells Samuel that he has obeyed God—well, almost. God had commanded him to destroy everything from the Amalekites, yet Saul spared King Agag's life and some of the animals. He blamed his soldiers, when in reality the problem was Saul's pride. He partially obeyed God.

Some claim to believe that the Bible is inspired, yet practice only some of what it requires. Like Jehoiakim, who cut out part of God's Word with his penknife and cast it into the fire (Jeremiah 36:23), they want only some (part) of God's Word, instead of the sum (all of it added together) of God's Word. In the denominational world, millions pledge allegiance to some verses but ignore others. Consider a few examples listed by B. J. Clarke:

- Many accept passages on faith but reject those that require water baptism for the remission of sins (Acts 2:38; 22:16; 1 Peter 3:21).

- Others praise the epistles but ignore what those epistles teach about the organization of the church with Christ as its sole Head and Legislator (Colossians 1:18). They ignore the qualifications for elders given in 1 Timothy 3 and Titus 1, substituting a board of deacons with a preacher as head in its place or allowing women to serve.

- Some believe in taking the Lord's supper, but ignore the pattern of frequency in Acts 20:7.

- Some believe in preaching and yet allow women to preach publicly. They accept Paul's teaching in 2 Timothy 4:1–5 but disregard his instructions in 1 Timothy 2:11–12.

- Many denominational groups preach "morality," while forming policies at conventions that allow homosexuals to be ministers, contrary to Romans 1:26–27 and 1 Corinthians 6:9–11.

Living the Christian life is not easy. Jesus said, "Come, take up the cross, and follow me" (Mark 10:21). He said we must strive to enter in at the strait gate (Luke 13:24; Matthew 7:13–14). Paul told the Ephesian elders that he had not shunned to declare to them the whole counsel of God (Acts 20:27). Obedience means doing all that God said.

Trust God. Obey God. Submit yourself each day to His will. Avoid the path of the prodigal by walking in the light with Jesus. The reward is salvation and peace today as well as eternal life to come.

And if you have wandered into the far country, thinking you would just have a little fun while you were young, it's not to late to come home. Your Father is waiting, eager to forgive.

Discussion Questions

1. What kind of scars does sin leave?

2. Why is Christianity a "better way" than worldly fun for Christian youth?

3. What is true obedience?

4. How do we develop trust in God?

5. Is it ever too late to come home from the prodigal life? Why or why not?

He Came to Himself

Lesson text: Luke 15

Memory verse: "I tell you, Nay: but, except ye repent, ye shall all likewise perish" (Luke 13:3).

When the prodigal son left for the far country, he probably didn't feel like a prodigal. He had money in his pocket; he had big dreams and big plans. He could hardly wait to escape his father's rules and his older brother's self-righteousness. The future looked bright. Filled with anticipation of adventure and new friends, he didn't give the home he was leaving a second thought.

Weeks passed, and months. He had a great time, especially in the early days of his sojourn in the far country. His new friends led him into all kinds of new experiences. Then his money ran out; his friends disappeared. Famine and hunger became his companions. He got a job slopping hogs—not exactly the kind of job he could brag about to his family. No man gave him anything, and he began to envy the hogs—at least they had food! (Luke 15:16).

One day, "he came to himself" (Luke 15:17). We might say he woke up and smelled the roses—or, in this case, the disgusting pigs! We might say the light bulb came on, or as he looked at his reflection in a pond, he wondered, "Who is that dirty, shabby person?" Perhaps a vision of home flashed through his mind. "How many hired servants of my father's have bread enough and to spare, and I perish with hunger!" (15:17).

"What am I doing here? I'll go home and confess my sins. I'll admit to my father that I'm not worthy to be called his son. Maybe, just maybe, he'll let me work as a servant; that's better than starving."

Remember the reunion scene? The prodigal son came limping home from the pigpen—penniless, smelly, hungry, penitent, and quite willing to accept punishment for his shameful, wasteful behavior. His father ran to greet him with hugs and kisses, and the son hardly finished half of his remorseful speech before his father threw a huge welcome-home party. The father had longed for this day. He had often looked down that empty road, hoping and praying that the prodigal would return. The lost son was finally found! (Luke 15:32). He had returned home sadder and wiser, having learned many hard lessons in the far country.

Modern Prodigals

Today, our world is filled with prodigal sons and daughters who waste the blessings God has given them. Some have never heard the gospel; they don't realize they are lost in the far country of sin. Others have been blessed to grow up in Christian homes and active congregations of the Lord's church, but they have decided to experiment with the prodigal lifestyle, or, as Luke called it, "riotous living" (Luke 15:13). Drinking, smoking, dancing, public swimming, sexual temptation, and questionable entertainment are sins that Satan presents in attractive ways.

We think we can try just a little and still be safe, but once we are in the far country, it's hard to return. Even if we come back and give up our prodigal ways, the price may be much higher than we ever expected to pay—a body damaged by alcohol and cigarettes or sexual disease; a baby we weren't ready to have, or even worse, the guilt of a hasty abortion; a reputation that makes it hard for those who love us to trust us again. Yes, God forgives; parents forgive. And, yes, we can do better, but consequences linger.

Ask Eve how one wrong decision can cause a lifetime of sorrow and regret. Ask Jonah how three days in a fish's belly will lead a stubborn heart to repentance. Ask David if his night of pleasure with Bathsheba was worth the guilt he felt for adultery, murder, and the loss of an innocent baby. Ask him about a son who raped his sister, and another son who murdered the rapist and later tried to take his father's throne. Ask Samson if his good times with Delilah were worth being blinded and humiliated.

Ask any prodigal today, "Was your sin worth the consequences?" If he has reached the pigpen, then he will say, "No. I really messed up my life." If she has any memory of how good she wanted her life to be, she will say, "No. I wish I had made better choices."

A Better Way

God provides a better way. Get to know God while you are young, and never leave His side. The Bible uses the phrase *know God* in the New Testament. It means that we have come to understand God's Word and are followers of it (1 John 2:3–5; Philippians 3:10; 2 Timothy 1:12). Many know about God but do not know God (Titus 1:16; cf. 1 Thessalonians 4:5; 2 Thessalonians 1:8).

The Prince of Granada was sentenced to Madrid's infamous prison, The Place of Skulls, in fear that he might aspire to the throne. For thirty-three years he remained in solitary confinement with but one book to read—the Bible. He read it hundreds of times. What did he say he learned?

- There are 3,538,483 letters in the Bible.
- The word *girl* appears once in the Bible (and *girls* once).
- No word or name of more than six syllables can be found in the Bible.
- The ninth verse of Esther 8 is the longest verse.

He knew all these things, but he never became a Christian. There is a difference between "head" knowledge and "heart" knowledge! It is a tragedy to spend hours and hours in study—or year after year in Bible class and worship—and not make any application of what we read and hear. John wrote, "And hereby we do know that we know him, if we keep his commandments" (1 John 2:3).

Full Tilt, All Out

A Japanese legend says a man died and went to heaven. On a sightseeing tour of his new home, he was shown all kinds of mansions—one built with marble and gold and precious stones, and another set in a lovely garden of lotus flowers. It was all beautiful, exactly as he had pictured it, until they came to what looked like a merchant's shop.

On the shelves were piled what looked like dried mushrooms. On closer examination, he saw they were actually human ears! His guide explained that these were the ears of those who went diligently to religious services, listened with pleasure, yet did nothing about what they heard, so only their ears went to heaven!

Samuel didn't just give God his ears. He dedicated his whole body, mind, and soul to serving God from his youth. He taught "all Israel" (1 Samuel 4:1), including the tough lessons about sincere repentance (1 Samuel 7:3). He prayed for the nation (7:5; 12:23). In his farewell speech to the Israelites after Saul became king, Samuel challenged the people to find fault with him. No one could honestly say that Samuel had ever taken a bribe or exalted himself. Everyone knew he was a man of God, fully committed to holiness (1 Samuel 12:2–5).

His success as a prophet and judge of God's people began with his childhood teaching and right choices as a youth. The Lord's half brother could have used Samuel as an example when he said, "Be ye doers of the word, and not hearers only, deceiving your own selves" (James 1:22). As Christians, we are not merely to speak well of all men; we are to do good unto all men (Galatians 6:10). We are not simply to ignore them that hate us; we are to do good unto them (Matthew 5:44). We are not to reflect on the beauty of faith, virtue, knowledge, temperance, steadfastness, godliness, brotherly affection and love; we are to practice these things (2 Peter 1:10). We are not to contemplate what we have seen, learned, received, and heard of the apostle Paul; we are to follow these things (Philippians 4:9; 1 Timothy 6:11).

Is it possible to follow God completely, even in the face of great temptations?

Ask Joseph, who refused to give in to sexual temptation. Although he was punished for something he didn't do, he triumphed in the end by becoming the second highest ruler in Egypt and eventually being reunited with his family. The Bible says that God was with him (Acts 7:9).

Ask Moses, who grew up in a palace yet chose poverty and service over riches and worldly power. The Bible says that God spoke to him as a man would speak to a friend (Exodus 33:11).

Ask Ruth, who chose God over idols, and service to her mother-in-law over her own family. The Bible lists her as the great-grandmother of King David and therefore an ancestor of Jesus (Ruth 4:17; Luke 3:23; 31–32).

Ask Samuel, a young man who answered, "Speak; for thy servant heareth," when God called him. The Bible records his successful roles as priest, prophet, judge, and king-maker for the nation of Israel (1 Samuel 1–25).

God still calls us today through His word, the Bible. Jesus came to earth to show us the better way, the way that brings us to God and saves us from the pain and despair of the far country of sin. Everybody needs the free gift that God provides—salvation through Christ (Romans 6:23; Ephesians 1:7). Do you have it? We urge you to give God your youth, your talents, your influence, and, most importantly, your heart.

Discussion Questions

1. What does it mean that the prodigal boy "came to himself"?

2. What would you say to a teen who says he can try a little sin and still be safe?

3. When God forgives, does He erase the consequences of sin, the guilt of sin, or both?

4. How do you think the prodigal boy would have answered the question: "Was your sin worth the consequences?"

5. What is a better way to experience the teen years than experimenting with sin?

6. Is it possible to remain faithful to God in the face of great temptations?

Samuel: A Young Man Who Got It Right

Lesson text: 1 Samuel 1, 3

Memory verse: "Remember now thy Creator in the days of thy youth, while the evil days come not, nor the years draw nigh, when thou shalt say, I have no pleasure in them" (Ecclesiastes 12:1).

We've talked about the strong man, Samson, who didn't always listen to God and make good choices. We've talked about David, who yielded to temptation and brought great suffering on himself and his family. Now let's consider Samuel, a young man who got it right.

Samuel's story begins with a woman named Hannah. Her husband, Elkanah, had taken a second wife who gave him children. Hannah wanted a son so much that she made a vow to God: She promised that if God would give her a son, she would give him into God's service (1 Samuel 1:11). God granted her request, and Hannah kept her vow, taking the child Samuel, whose name means, "asked of the Lord" (1 Samuel 1:20), to live with Eli in Shiloh and be trained in the ways of the priesthood. Samuel became a great priest, prophet, and judge who judged Israel "all the days of his life" (1 Samuel 7:15).

You may be thinking, "Samuel didn't have a choice; his mother made him become a priest!" But God created all people with the ability to choose; we call it free will. Without free will, we would all be nice, obedient robots. Yes, God wants us to obey His commandments, but He wants us to obey out of love, not because we have no choice.

In a way, Samuel was a prime candidate to become a prodigal child. He grew up in the tabernacle, seeing his parents only once a year (1 Samuel 2:19). He practiced priestly duties while still a boy, tutored by Eli (1 Samuel 2:11, 18; 3:1). He knew a lot about God before he knew God (1 Samuel 3:7).

He also saw the bad example set by Eli's sons, Hophni and Phinehas (1 Samuel 2:12–17, 22–25). It would have been easy for Samuel to say, "If Eli's sons can get away with sin, why can't I?" Or, "I know Mom and Dad expect me to be a priest, but I want to see for myself what the real world is like. I'll be a priest later." He could have complained. He could have rebelled.

But he didn't. Samuel chose to fulfill the plans that his mother made for him. He chose to obey Eli, although Eli's own sons disobeyed him. Most of all, Samuel chose to obey God. In fact, the Bible records only one serious regret in Samuel's life: His own sons didn't honor God (1 Samuel 8:1–3). They failed to follow their father's example of obedience. Sadly, he had more influence on the nation of Israel than he had on his family.

Let's consider some lessons we can learn from Samuel's story.

Lesson #1: A Flower Can Grow in a Desert (1 Samuel 3:1)

Samuel lived during a sad time in Israel. True religion was unpopular, and "every man did that which was right in his own eyes" (Judges 17:6; 21:25). Samuel saw firsthand that even priests could be corrupt (1 Samuel 2:12–18).

Yet in this desert grew a young flower. The boy Samuel grew in favor with God and man (1 Samuel 2:26; cf. Luke 2:52). A little later, when God called Samuel in the night, this young man answered, "Speak; for thy servant heareth" (1 Samuel 3:10). Samuel continued to grow and listen to God; eventually all of Israel recognized him as a prophet because he spoke what God revealed to him (1 Samuel 3:19–21).

Samuel is proof that a godly life can develop in spite of ungodly influences surrounding it, but he is not the only young person in the Bible who made good choices. Consider these examples:

- Moses lived among pagans as a boy in Egypt, but he chose rather to suffer with the people of God than to enjoy the pleasures of sin for a season (Hebrews 11:25).

- Ruth was a young widow who chose to take care of her mother-in-law, Naomi, and obey her God instead of returning to the idolatry of her own people (Ruth 1:16–17).

- Daniel was pressured to worship false gods as a captive in Babylon, but he purposed in his heart that he would not defile himself (Daniel 1:8).

- Jesus grew up as a tender plant in Nazareth, a place that had a reputation that prompted Nathanael to ask, "Can there any good thing come out of Nazareth?" (John 1:46; cf. Isaiah 53:2). Yet He remained sinless all of His life (Hebrews 4:15).

What about young people today? Can they stay home instead of following the prodigal's path? More important, what about you? Will you chose to be a Samuel or a Samson?

You may not have the best circumstances in which to serve God. You may have to attend a school where it seems everybody but you is following the devil's ways. You may have to go to church services by yourself or get a grandparent or friend to take you because you do not have Christian parents. You may go with a mother who serves God but have a father who discourages you from being a Christian. Your family may be confusing you because it is divided with one parent attending the church of Christ (Romans 16:16) and another attending a denomination.

Even if everyone in your family attends church with you, other conditions may be less than perfect. You may attend a congregation that has a poor youth program or one that does not have any other Christians your age. Worse, you may have found that some of the teens only pretend to be Christians and are living sinful lives when they are away from their parents and fellow church members. Samuel was probably discouraged at times, especially when he saw the hypocrisy of Eli's sons. Maybe he wondered, "How can I do what's right when even God's priests are disobedient?" Maybe he even thought about giving up. But he didn't.

Should you give up? Do you have to be a weak Christian because you do not have ideal circumstances? No! Instead, you'll just have to be like Samuel and grow like a flower in the desert. God can still use you to do great things in His kingdom.

Samuel was not isolated from his sinful world (Matthew 9:10), but he was separated from it (2 Corinthians 6:17; James 4:4). He could not keep from being in the world, but he could keep the world from being in him. He came in contact with sin, yet did not allow himself to be contaminated by it. He made up his mind not to be polluted with the sin around him (2 Peter 2:20–22). He was a "living sacrifice," transformed by the renewing of his mind (Romans 12:1–2). Samuel looked at Hophni and Phinehas, and he chose to be different. He listened to Eli, and he listened to God. He honored his mother's vow. "And the Lord appeared again in Shiloh: for the Lord revealed himself to Samuel (1 Samuel 3:21).

It seems that God gets His greatest workers from two opposite groups. Paul, who went from persecutor to apostle, heads one class. He was so grateful to be forgiven of so many sins that he worked more diligently than others (1 Corinthians 15:9–10). This kind of servant is often more earnest, humble, and wholehearted because of the memory of wasted youth and of God's mercy.

Samuel and Timothy represent the other class (Acts 16:1; 1 Corinthians 4:17; 2 Timothy 3:15). These men made great workers for God at least in part because they had so little sin and so few bad habits to overcome from their pre-Christian lives. It is good to have much transgression forgiven, but it is better to have always been innocent and ignorant of it (1 Corinthians 14:20). At the best, years are squandered which do not return (James 4:14). At worst, habits have taken hold for which one will eventually trade eternal life (Romans 6:14–16; cf. Ecclesiastes 12:1).

Young person, be like Samuel; grow up "in the nurture and admonition of the Lord" (Ephesians 6:4), and escape the scars and sorrows of a life wrongly begun. Don't experiment with sin—even if you later forsake it, it will likely leave you tainted and scarred. Sinful behavior leaves traces of itself on the soul. You'll never regret sins you don't commit; you'll likely come to regret every sin you commit.

Lesson #2: There Comes an Age of Accountability in Every Person's Life (1 Samuel 3:1)

Whatever was the age of Samuel's accountability, he had reached it, and God now held him responsible. At some point, all young people must make personal decisions for Christ.

How old was Samuel? The term *child* or *boy* as used here can be applied to an infant (1 Samuel 4:21) or to a man forty years old (2 Chronicles 13:7). The Jewish historian Josephus says that Samuel's call happened when he had just completed his twelfth year. That was the age the Jews traditionally held Bar-Mitzvah services for boys. Entering the thirteenth year, a Jewish boy became a "Son of the Law," when he was held responsible for his behavior and was morally and ethically considered an adult. Many believe that it was upon this occasion that Jesus Christ was left by his parents in Jerusalem (Luke 2:41–51).

What is the age of accountability today? The age of accountability comes at different ages for different young people (some mature faster than others), but two passages give guidelines. First, when Jesus was twelve years old, He was "about [His] Father's business" (Luke 2:42, 49). Second, God used twenty as the cut-off point when he forbade Israel to enter the Promised Land because of unbelief (Numbers 14:29).

Thus, we can easily narrow it to the teen years. In general, when one knows the difference between right and wrong, he or she has reached the age of accountability and should be baptized (Acts 2:38; 22:16) and start serving God faithfully (Revelation 2:10). For most, such knowledge comes between the ages of twelve and fifteen.

Lesson #3: We Must Not Refuse to Come When God Calls (1 Samuel 3:4)

Samuel lived during a time of miracles, so God spoke directly to him. God does not call people like that today (1 Corinthians 13:8–10), but God does call people today. The denominational world is wrong when it tells young people to listen for God's voice in the night or for some direct operation of the Holy Spirit, but we are right to tell you that God is calling you right now to be a Christian. The Corinthians were "called to be saints, with all that in every place call upon the name of Jesus Christ our Lord, both theirs and ours" (1 Corinthians 1:2). How does God call us? Through His Word: "Whereunto he called you by our gospel" (2 Thessalonians 2:14).

When Hitler's number two Nazi, Hermann Goering, was placed in prison awaiting execution, a prison chaplain visited him to talk about preparing to meet God. Goering ridiculed the Bible and refused to accept that Christ died for sinners. He denied the power of Christ's blood. "Death is death," was the substance of his last words. As the chaplain mentioned that he might one day see his little daughter in heaven, he replied, "She believes in her manner, I in mine." The chaplain left discouraged. Less than an hour later Goering committed suicide.

God called this man through His Word, but he refused to answer (Proverbs 29:1). God calls to us by the same Bible. It is not just the preacher or our parents or our friends, but God who is calling us to His church. We can, of course, resist and rebel and reject until our conscience becomes seared with a hot iron (1 Timothy 4:2). Cain, Balaam, Samson, Korah, and Ahab all reached a day when they turned their backs on God—and we can, too (cf. Acts 24:25; 26:28). God wants all young people to enlist in His service (1 Samuel 3:10). Don't wait too long to heed the gospel call!

Like Samuel and Timothy, you can choose to avoid the prodigal's path. You can choose obedience and faithfulness and service to God all your life. What better time to begin than when you are young? What better time than *now?* (2 Corinthians 6:2).

Why not be a prodigal? Sin will teach you more than you want to know, take you farther than you want to go, keep you longer than you want to stay, and cost you more than you want to pay.

Stay home.

Discussion Questions

1. What does it mean to "remember now thy Creator in the days of thy youth"? How did Samuel follow this advice? How can teens follow it today?

2. What bad circumstances could have influenced Samuel? What bad circumstances may influence Christian teens today? How can you overcome bad circumstances and be faithful to God?

3. Consider the negative influences in the lives of Moses, Ruth, and Daniel. What choices did they make?

4. We often emphasize that Jesus never sinned; we may forget that he chose not to sin. Hebrews 4:15 tells us Jesus was tempted just as we are today, but He did not sin. How did Jesus overcome temptation? (Matthew 4:1–11).

5. How does a person know when he has reached the age of accountability?

6. How do people hear the call of God today?

7. What is the difference between knowing about God and knowing God?

8. We often remind young people that they must be "in the world but not of the world." Is it possible for a person to be "in the church but not of the church"? How? What should teens do to avoid this problem?

9. What are the advantages of knowing God from a young age?

10. What is your favorite chapter of this book? What are some things you want to remember from this class?

ENDNOTES:

[1] http://jurongsda.org/aboutgod/aboutgod.htm.

[2] http://www.hup.harvard.edu/catalog/GINGOD.html?show=reviews.

[3] http://www.leaderu.com/real/ri9403/evidence.html.

[4] http://academic.brooklyn.cuny.edu/history/virtual/reading/core4-04r06.htm.

[5] http://www.xmission.com/~fidelis/volume3/chapter26/tributes.php.

[6] http://www.xmission.com/~fidelis/volume3/chapter26/tributes.php.

[7] http://shakespeare.about.com/library/weekly/aa101000a.htm.

[8] http://www.chuckbaldwinlive.com/founding.html#gw.

[9] http://www.eadshome.com/JohnAdams.htm.

[10] http://www.congress.gov.ph/legis/print_journal.php?congress=13&id=126.

[11] http://www.bible.org/page.php?page_id=3450.

[12] http://forerunner.com/forerunner/X0205_John_Quincy_Adams.html.

[13] http://www.tentmaker.org/Quotes/biblequotes.htm.

[14] http://www.columbia.edu/cu/augustine/arch/chr_heritage.html.

[15] http://jcsm.org/AmericasFounders/WilliamPenn.htm.

[16] http://www.bibleintheschools.org/www/docs/119.52.

[17] http://www.av1611.org/jmelton/kjvstuff.html.

[18] http://www.thescriptures.org/quotes/index.html.